**GRADE 4B**

# Student Book

**Consultant and Author**
Dr. Fong Ho Kheong

**Authors**
Chelvi Ramakrishnan and Gan Kee Soon

**U.S. Consultants**
Dr. Richard Bisk
Andy Clark
Patsy F. Kanter

**Marshall Cavendish**
Education

U.S. Distributor

**Houghton
Mifflin
Harcourt**

© 2018 Marshall Cavendish Education Pte Ltd

**Published by Marshall Cavendish Education**
Times Centre, 1 New Industrial Road, Singapore 536196
Customer Service Hotline: (65) 6213 9444
US Office Tel: (1-914) 332 8888 | Fax: (1-914) 332 8882
E-mail: tmesales@mceducation.com
Website: www.mceducation.com

Distributed by
**Houghton Mifflin Harcourt**
222 Berkeley Street
Boston, MA 02116
Tel: 617-351-5000
Website: www.hmheducation.com/mathinfocus

Cover: © Krys Bailey/Alamy,
© Tom Uhlman/Alamy.
Images provided by Houghton Mifflin Harcourt.

First published 2018

ISBN 978-1-328-88087-1

Printed in the United States of America

3  4  5  6  7  8          1401          23  22  21  20  19  18
4500690547                              A  B  C  D  E

# Contents

 Decimals

Look for **Practice and Problem Solving**

| Student Book A and Student Book B | Workbook A and Workbook B |
|---|---|
| • **Let's Practice** in every lesson | • **Independent Practice** for every lesson |
| • **Put On Your Thinking Cap!** in every chapter | • **Put On Your Thinking Cap!** in every chapter |

Look for **Assessment Opportunities**

| Student Book A and Student Book B | Workbook A and Workbook B |
|---|---|
| • **Quick Check** at the beginning of every chapter to assess chapter readiness | • **Cumulative Reviews** six times during the year |
| • **Guided Learning** after every example or two to assess readiness to continue lesson | • **Mid-Year and End-of-Year Reviews** to assess test readiness |
| • **Chapter Review/Test** in every chapter to review or test chapter material | |

# 8 Adding and Subtracting Decimals

 **Angles**

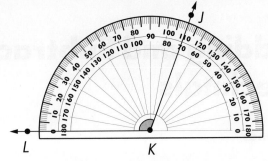

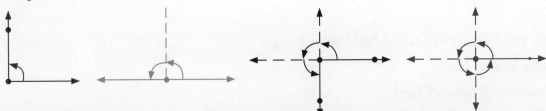

# 10 Perpendicular and Parallel Line Segments

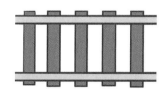

# Squares and Rectangles

# 12 Conversion of Measurements

# Area and Perimeter

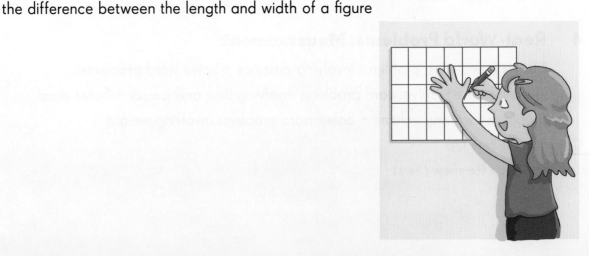

# Symmetry

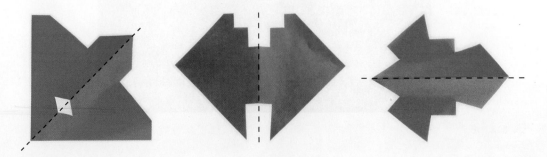

# Tessellations

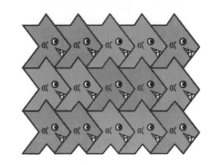

# Welcome to
# Math in Focus®

This exciting math program comes to you all the way from the country of Singapore. We are sure you will enjoy learning math with the interesting lessons you'll find in these books.

## What makes *Math in Focus*® different?

▶ **Two books** You don't write in the ▢ in this textbook. This book has a matching **Workbook**. When you see the pencil icon 👤 **ON YOUR OWN** ✏️, you will write in the **Workbook**.

▶ **Longer lessons** Some lessons may last more than a day, so you can really understand the math.

▶ **Math will make sense** Learn to use bar models to solve word problems with ease.

## In this book, look for

| Learn | Guided Learning | Let's Practice | 👤 ON YOUR OWN ✏️ |
|---|---|---|---|
| This means you will learn something new. | Your teacher will help you try some sample problems. | You practice what you've learned to solve more problems. You can make sure you really understand. | Now you get to practice with lots of different problems in your own **Workbook**. |

**Also look forward to** *Games, Hands-On Activities, Math Journals, Let's Explore,* and *Put On Your Thinking Cap!*
You will combine logical thinking with math skills and concepts to meet new problem-solving challenges. You will be talking math, thinking math, doing math, and even writing about doing math.

# What's in the Workbook?

*Math in Focus*®will give you time to learn important new concepts and skills and check your understanding. Then you will use the practice pages in the **Workbook** to try:

▶ Solving different problems to practice the new math concept you are learning. In the textbook, keep an eye open for this symbol **ON YOUR OWN**. That will tell you which pages to use for practice.

▶ *Put On Your Thinking Cap!*

  *Challenging Practice* problems invite you to think in new ways to solve harder problems.

  *Problem Solving* challenges you to use different strategies to solve problems.

▶ Math Journal activities ask you to think about thinking, and then write about that!

Students in Singapore have been using this kind of math program for many years. Now you can too — are you ready?

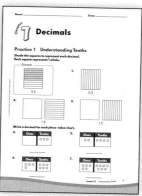

# 7 Decimals

$1.20 each

$2.56 each

$0.99 each

Fresh Fruit

The weight of the watermelon is between 14.0 pounds and 14.5 pounds.

This weighing scale gives a more accurate reading. The weight of the watermelon is 14.37 pounds.

## Lessons

## BIG IDEAS

▶ Decimals are another way to show amounts that are parts of a whole.

▶ A decimal has a decimal point to the right of the ones place and digits to the right of the decimal point.

## Recall Prior Knowledge

**Knowing fractions with a denominator of 10**

The shaded parts show $\frac{3}{10}$. Read $\frac{3}{10}$ as three tenths.

**Knowing mixed numbers with a denominator of 10**

The shaded parts show $\frac{23}{10}$ or $2\frac{3}{10}$. Read $2\frac{3}{10}$ as two and three tenths.

**Expressing fractions as equivalent fractions with a denominator of 10, and simplifying fractions with a denominator of 10**

$$\frac{3}{5} = \frac{6}{10}$$

(×2, ×2)

$$\frac{8}{10} = \frac{4}{5}$$

(÷2, ÷2)

Multiply the numerator and denominator by the same number.

Divide the numerator and denominator by the same number.

**2**    **Chapter 7**  Decimals

## Rounding numbers to the nearest ten

When the ones digit is 0, 1, 2, 3, or 4, round the number to the lesser ten.

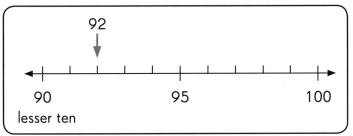

92 is nearer to 90 than to 100.

92 is about 90.

When the ones digit is 5, 6, 7, 8, or 9, round the number to the greater ten.

47 is nearer to 50 than to 40.

47 is about 50.

## ✔ Quick Check

**Find the fraction or mixed number shown by the shaded parts.**

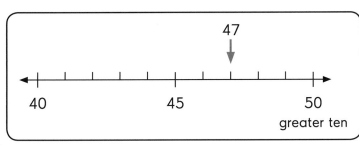

**Find each missing numerator and denominator.**

 $\dfrac{1}{5} = \dfrac{\boxed{\phantom{0}}}{10}$

4  $\dfrac{5}{10} = \dfrac{1}{\boxed{\phantom{0}}}$

5  $\dfrac{4}{10} = \dfrac{2}{\boxed{\phantom{0}}}$

**Round to the nearest ten.**

 25

7  107

# 7.1 Understanding Tenths

## Lesson Objectives

- Read and write tenths in decimal and fractional forms.
- Represent and interpret tenths models.

**Vocabulary**
tenth
decimal form
decimal point
expanded form

**Learn** **Express fractions in tenths as decimals.**

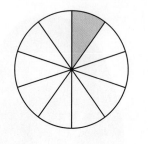

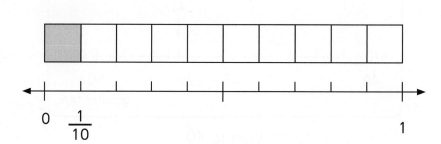

$0 \quad \dfrac{1}{10}$ 　　　　　　　　　　　　　　　　　　　1

Each part is $\dfrac{1}{10}$ (one tenth).

Write $\dfrac{1}{10}$ as 0.1 in **decimal form**.

0.1 is 1 tenth written in decimal form.

0.1

↑

**decimal point**

Read 0.1 as one tenth.
Its value is 1 tenth.

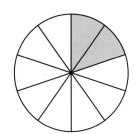
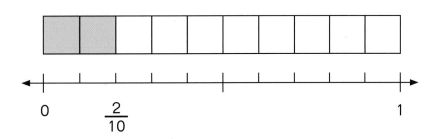

Two parts out of ten is $\frac{2}{10}$ (two tenths).

Write $\frac{2}{10}$ as 0.2 in decimal form.

In the same way, I can write $\frac{3}{10}$ as 0.3 and $\frac{4}{10}$ as 0.4.

Just like the fractions $\frac{1}{10}$ and $\frac{2}{10}$,

0.1 and 0.2 are parts of a whole.

0.1 and 0.2 are called decimals.

A decimal is a number with a decimal point, and digits to the right of the decimal point.

## Guided Learning

### Express each of these as a decimal.

**1** $\frac{5}{10}$ = 

**2** $\frac{6}{10}$ = 

**3** 3 tenths = 

**4** eight tenths = 

### Find the decimals that the shaded and unshaded parts represent.

**5** 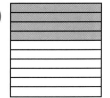  shaded parts: 

unshaded parts: 

**6**   shaded parts: 

unshaded parts:

# Find the decimal for each point on the number line.

**7**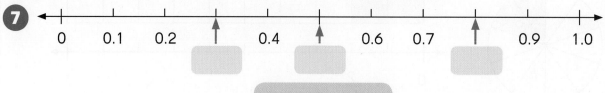

0    0.1    0.2         0.4         0.6    0.7         0.9    1.0

0.5 is $\frac{5}{10}$ or $\frac{1}{2}$.

---

**Learn** **Find equivalent ones and tenths.**

| Ones | Tenths |
|------|--------|
|      | ⦿⦿⦿⦿⦿ ⦿⦿⦿⦿⦿ |

| Ones | Tenths |
|------|--------|
| ⦿    |        |

$\frac{10}{10}$ is equal to 1.

10 tenths $=$ 1 one

You can regroup 10 tenths as 1 one.

---

**Learn** **Express mixed numbers as decimals.**

Rewrite $1\frac{6}{10}$ as a decimal.

| Ones | Tenths |
|------|--------|
| ⦿    | ⦿⦿⦿ ⦿⦿⦿ |
| 1    | 6      |

$1\frac{6}{10}$ $=$ 1 one and 6 tenths

      $=$ 1.6

The word 'and' tells you where to put the decimal point. Read 1.6 as one and six tenths.

**Express improper fractions as decimals.**

Rewrite $\frac{12}{10}$ as a decimal.

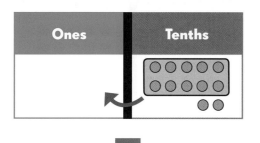

| Ones | Tenths |
|------|--------|
|      | ○○○○○ ○○○○○ |
|      | ○○ |

$\frac{12}{10} = 12$ tenths

2 tenths

10 tenths $= 1$ one

$\frac{12}{10} = 1$ one and 2 tenths

$= 1.2$

| Ones | Tenths |
|------|--------|
| ○    | ○○     |
| 1    | 2      |

Decimals are another way of writing fractions and mixed numbers.

## Guided Learning

**Express each of these as a decimal.**

**8** 15 tenths =

**9** 2 ones and 3 tenths =

**Find the decimals that the shaded parts represent.**

**10**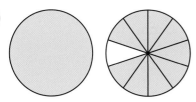

**11**

**Look at the points marked X on the number line.**
**Find the decimals that these points represent.**

**12**

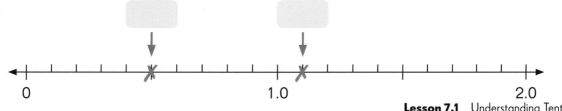

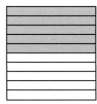

**Express each of these as a decimal.**

**13**

| Ones | Tenths |
|------|--------|
| ●● | ●●● ●●● |

[          ]

**14**

| Ones | Tenths |
|------|--------|
| | ●●●● ●●●● ●●●● ●●●● ●● |

[          ]

**15** $2\frac{9}{10}$ = [          ]

**16** $\frac{27}{10}$ = [          ]

**Express the length of each insect as a fraction and a decimal.**

**Example**

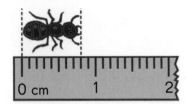

Length of ant  $= \frac{8}{10}$ cm

$= 0.8$ cm

**17**

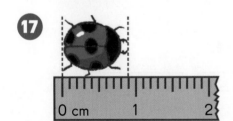

Length of ladybug  $= \dfrac{[\ ]}{10}$ cm

$= [\quad]$ cm

**18**

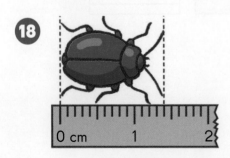

Length of beetle  $= [\quad]$ cm

$= [\quad]$ cm

**Express the total amount of water as a mixed number and a decimal.**

19

Total amount of water = $1\dfrac{\boxed{\phantom{0}}}{\boxed{\phantom{0}}}$ L

= $\boxed{\phantom{000}}$ L

**Express each decimal as tenths.**

20 0.9 = $\boxed{\phantom{00}}$ tenths

21 0.7 = $\boxed{\phantom{00}}$ tenths

22 1.1 = $\boxed{\phantom{00}}$ tenths

23 4.3 = $\boxed{\phantom{00}}$ tenths

**Learn** **Write decimals to show their place values.**

| Tens | Ones | Tenths |
|:---:|:---:|:---:|
| 4 | 2 | 3 |

42.3 = 4 tens + 2 ones + 3 tenths
     = 40 + 2 + 0.3
     = 40 + 2 + $\dfrac{3}{10}$

$40 + 2 + \dfrac{3}{10}$ is called the **expanded form** of a decimal.

## Guided Learning

**Find the missing numbers in expanded form.**

24 76.4 = $\boxed{\phantom{00}}$ tens + $\boxed{\phantom{00}}$ ones + $\boxed{\phantom{00}}$ tenths

= 70 + 6 + $\boxed{\phantom{00}}$

= 70 + 6 + $\dfrac{\boxed{\phantom{0}}}{10}$

**Use place value to understand whole number and decimal amounts.**

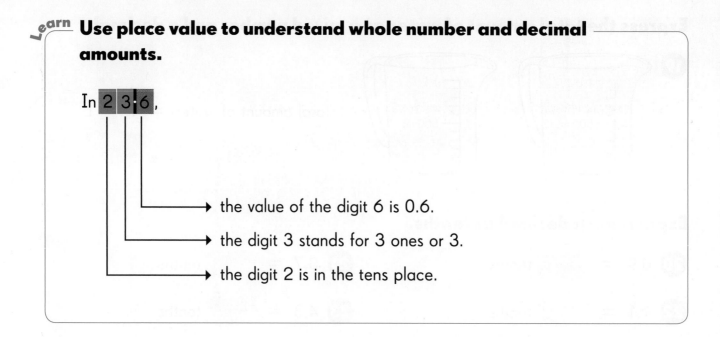

In 2 3.6,

→ the value of the digit 6 is 0.6.

→ the digit 3 stands for 3 ones or 3.

→ the digit 2 is in the tens place.

## Guided Learning

**Find the missing numbers.**

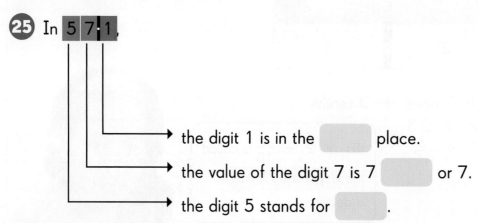

25 In 5 7.1,

the digit 1 is in the ▢ place.

the value of the digit 7 is 7 ▢ or 7.

the digit 5 stands for ▢.

26 In 49.8, the digit ▢ is in the tenths place.

27 In 95.6, the digit 5 stands for ▢.

28 In 50.2, the value of the digit 0 is ▢.

29 In 92.9, the two digits 9 stand for ▢ and ▢.

# Let's Practice

**Find the decimals that the shaded parts represent.**

**1**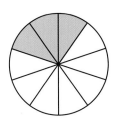

$\dfrac{\boxed{\phantom{0}}}{10}$ = $\boxed{\phantom{000}}$

**2**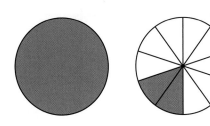

$1\dfrac{\boxed{\phantom{0}}}{10}$ = $\boxed{\phantom{000}}$

**Copy the number line. Mark ✗ to show where each decimal is located.**

**3** 0.7

0          1.0          2.0

**4** 1.1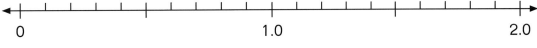

0          1.0          2.0

**Express each of these as a decimal.**

**5**

| Ones | Tenths |
|------|--------|
| ○ ○ | ○○○○○ ○○○ |

$\boxed{\phantom{000}}$

**6**

| Ones | Tenths |
|------|--------|
|  | ○○○○○ ○○○○○ ○○○○ |

$\boxed{\phantom{000}}$

**7** $\dfrac{4}{10}$ m = $\boxed{\phantom{000}}$ m

**8** 7 tenths = $\boxed{\phantom{000}}$

**9** $\dfrac{16}{10}$ L = $\boxed{\phantom{000}}$ L

**10** 14 tenths = $\boxed{\phantom{000}}$

**11** $2\dfrac{9}{10}$ kg = $\boxed{\phantom{000}}$ kg

**12** 9 ones and 6 tenths = $\boxed{\phantom{000}}$

**Express each decimal as tenths.**

**13** 0.3 = [ ] tenths

**14** 2.9 = [ ] tenths

**Find the missing numbers.**

**15** 3.5 = 3 ones and [ ] tenths

**16** 18.7 = [ ] ten 8 ones and [ ] tenths

**17** 7.5 = 7 + [ ]

**18** 10.8 = [ ] + 0.8

**19** 3.6 = 3 + $\frac{6}{\boxed{\phantom{0}}}$

**20** 21.4 = [ ] + [ ] + $\frac{\boxed{\phantom{0}}}{10}$

**Find the missing words or numbers.**

| Tens | Ones | Tenths |
|------|------|--------|
| 3 | 7 • | 5 |

**21** The digit 7 is in the [ ] place.

**22** The digit 3 stands for [ ].

**23** The value of the digit 5 is [ ].

ON YOUR OWN

Go to Workbook B:
Practice 1, pages 1–4

# 7.2 Understanding Hundredths

## Lesson Objectives

* Read and write hundredths in decimal and fractional forms.
* Represent and interpret hundredths models.

**Vocabulary**
hundredth

placeholder zero

**Learn** **Express fractions in hundredths as decimals.**

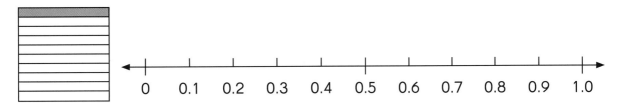

The square and the number line are each divided into 10 parts.
Each part is 1 tenth.

Divide each tenth into 10 parts.
Now the square and number line each have 100 equal parts.

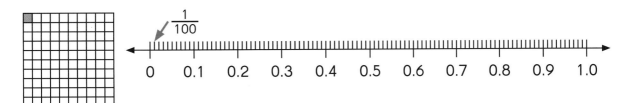

Each part is $\frac{1}{100}$ (one hundredth).

Write $\frac{1}{100}$ as 0.01 in decimal form.

$0.01 = \frac{1}{100}$
Read 0.01 as one hundredth.
Its value is 1 hundredth.

In the same way, write $\frac{2}{100}$ as 0.02 and $\frac{3}{100}$ as 0.03.

## Guided Learning

### Express each of these as a decimal.

**1** $\frac{4}{100}$ oz = [ ] oz

**2** $\frac{6}{100}$ in. = [ ] in.

**3** five hundredths = [ ]

**4** 8 hundredths = [ ]

### Find the decimals that the shaded parts represent.

**5**  [ ]

**6** [ ]

### Find the decimal for each point on the number line.

**7**

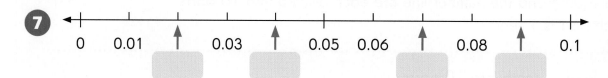

0    0.01    [ ]    0.03    [ ]    0.05    0.06    [ ]    0.08    [ ]    0.1

### ᴸᵉᵃʳⁿ Find equivalent tenths and hundredths.

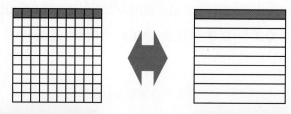

| Tenths | Hundredths |
|--------|------------|
|        | ●●●●● ●●●●● |

| Tenths | Hundredths |
|--------|------------|
| ●      |            |

$\frac{10}{100}$ is equal to $\frac{1}{10}$ or 0.1.

10 hundredths = 1 tenth

You can regroup 10 hundredths as 1 tenth.

**Express tenths and hundredths as decimals.**

What is 2 tenths 5 hundredths written as a decimal?

| Ones | | Tenths | Hundredths |
|------|---|--------|------------|
| | | ● ● | ● ● ●<br>● ● |
| 0 | • | 2 | 5 |

2 tenths **+** 5 hundredths **=** 0.25

0.25 is twenty-five hundredths.

**Express fractions as decimals.**

Rewrite $\frac{15}{100}$ as a decimal.

$$\frac{15}{100} = 15 \text{ hundredths}$$

10 hundredths **=** 1 tenth

5 hundredths

| Ones | | Tenths | Hundredths |
|------|---|--------|------------|
| | | | ○ ○ ○ ○ ○<br>○ ○ ○ ○ ○<br>○ ○ ○ ○ ○ |

| Ones | | Tenths | Hundredths |
|------|---|--------|------------|
| | | ● | ○ ○ ○ ○ ○ |
| 0 | • | 1 | 5 |

$\frac{15}{100}$ = 1 tenth + 5 hundredths

= 0.1 + 0.05

= 0.15

## Guided Learning

**Express each of these as a decimal.**

**8** 14 hundredths = [ ]

**9** 3 tenths 2 hundredths = [ ]

**Find the decimals that the shaded parts represent.**

**10** 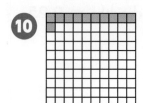 [ ]

**11** 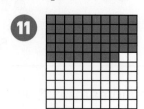 [ ]

**Look at the points marked ✗ on the number line.**
**Find the decimals that these points represent.**

**12** [ ]  [ ]

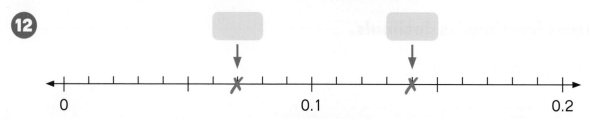

**Express each of these as a decimal.**

**13**

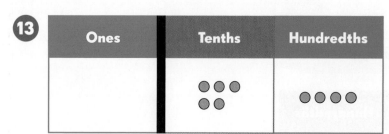

[ ]

**14**

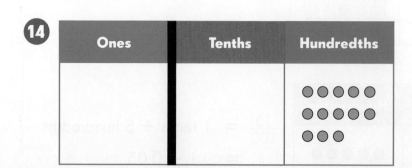

[ ]

A tenth of a tenth is a hundredth.

**15** $\frac{21}{100}$ = [ ]

**16** $\frac{87}{100}$ = [ ]

**Decimals can have placeholder zeros.**

Does 0.90 have the same value as 0.9?

$0.90 = \dfrac{90}{100}$

$= \dfrac{9}{10}$

$= 0.9$

$$\dfrac{90}{100} = \dfrac{9}{10}$$

÷ 10

÷ 10

_Learn_ **Express ones, tenths, and hundredths as decimals.**

What is 2 ones and 4 tenths 7 hundredths written as a decimal?

| Ones | Tenths | Hundredths |
|------|--------|------------|
| ● ● | ● ● ● ● | ● ● ● ● ● ● ● |

2 ones and 4 tenths 7 hundredths
= 2 ones and 47 hundredths
= 2.47

## Guided Learning

**Express each of these as a decimal.**

**17**

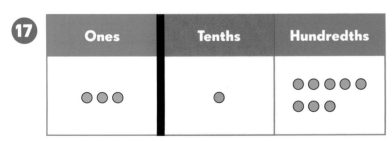

| Ones | Tenths | Hundredths |
|------|--------|------------|
| ● ● ● | ● | ● ● ● ● ● ● ● ● |

**18**  4 ones and 9 tenths 1 hundredth =

## Find the decimal that the shaded parts represent.

 **19**

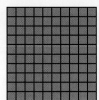 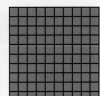 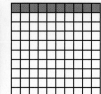 

## Look at the points marked X on the number line.
## Find the decimals that these points represent.

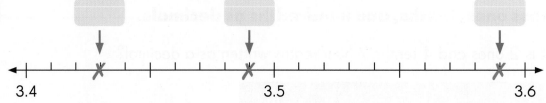

**20**

3.4          3.5          3.6

---

*Learn* **Express mixed numbers as decimals.**

Rewrite $1\frac{53}{100}$ as a decimal.

| Ones | | Tenths | Hundredths |
|---|---|---|---|
| ● | | ● ● ● ● ● | ● ● ● |
| 1 | ● | 5 | 3 |

$1\frac{53}{100}$ = 1 one and 5 tenths 3 hundredths
      = 1 one and 53 hundredths
      = 1.53

---

*Learn* **Express improper fractions as decimals.**

Rewrite $\frac{147}{100}$ as a decimal.

$\frac{147}{100}$ = 1 one and 47 hundredths
      = 1.47

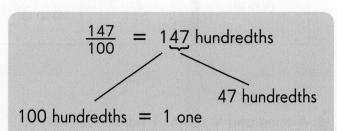

$\frac{147}{100}$ = 147 hundredths

100 hundredths = 1 one          47 hundredths

---

## Guided Learning

**Express each fraction or mixed number as a decimal.**

**21** $2\frac{75}{100}$ = ☐

**22** $\frac{103}{100}$ = ☐

**23** $3\frac{16}{100}$ L = ☐ L

**24** $\frac{204}{100}$ km = ☐ km

**Express each decimal as hundredths.**

**25** 0.03 = ☐ hundredths

**26** 0.31 = ☐ hundredths

**27** 6.17 = ☐ hundredths

**28** 2.09 = ☐ hundredths

### Learn Write decimals to show their place values.

| Tens | Ones | | Tenths | Hundredths |
|------|------|---|--------|------------|
| 7 | 8 | • | 4 | 1 |

$78.41 = 7$ tens $+ 8$ ones $+ 4$ tenths $+ 1$ hundredth

$= 70 + 8 + 0.4 + 0.01$

$= 70 + 8 + \frac{4}{10} + \frac{1}{100}$

## Guided Learning

**Find the missing numbers in the expanded form.**

**29** $20.39$ = ☐ tens $+$ ☐ ones $+$ ☐ tenths $+$ ☐ hundredths

$= 20 + 0.3 +$ ☐

$= 20 + \frac{☐}{10} + \frac{☐}{100}$

# Learn Use place value to understand whole number and decimal amounts.

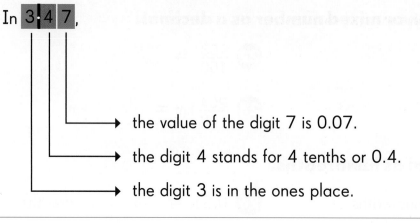

In 3.47,

→ the value of the digit 7 is 0.07.

→ the digit 4 stands for 4 tenths or 0.4.

→ the digit 3 is in the ones place.

## Guided Learning

**Find the missing words or numbers.**

**30** In 5.18, the digit 1 is in the ⬜ place.

**31** In 2.59, the value of the digit 9 is ⬜ .

**32** In 82.03, the value of the digit 8 is ⬜ .

# Learn Use decimals to write dollars and cents.

One dollar → $1.00 = 100¢

17¢ = $0.17        70¢ = $0.70        7¢ = $0.07

## Guided Learning

**Express each amount using a dollar sign and decimal point.**

**33** 53¢ = $ [ ]          **34** 30¢ = $ [ ]          **35** 3¢ = $ [ ]

**Express each amount in decimal form.**

**Example**
3 dollars and 25 cents = $3.25

> A cent is $\frac{1}{100}$ of a dollar.

**36** 7 dollars and 40 cents = $ [ ]          **37** 18 dollars = $ [ ]

**38** 33 dollars and 5 cents = $ [ ]

## Let's Practice

**Find the decimals that the shaded parts represent.**

**1** 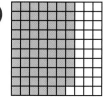 [ ]

**2**  [ ]

**Look at the point marked X on each number line.**
**Find the decimals that these points represent.**

**3**

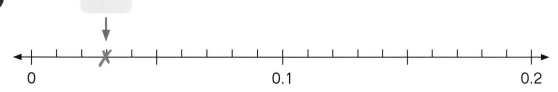

**4**

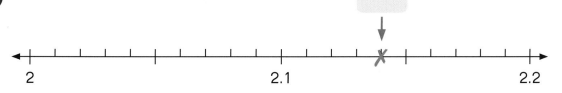

**Copy each number line. Mark X to show where each decimal is located.**

**5** 0.08

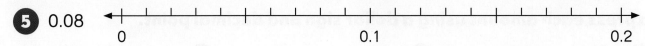

0        0.1        0.2

**6** 0.76

0.7        0.8        0.9

**7** 3.45

3.3        3.4        3.5

**Express each of these as a decimal.**

**8**

| Ones | Tenths | Hundredths |
|------|--------|------------|
|      | ● ● ●  | ● ● ● ● ●  |

**9**

| Ones | Tenths | Hundredths |
|------|--------|------------|
| ● ●  | ● ● ● ● ● ● | ● ● ● ● ● ● ● ● ● ● |

**10** $\frac{35}{100}$ lb = [    ] lb

**11** 3 L = [    ] L

**12** $\frac{308}{100}$ mi = [    ] mi

**13** $\frac{61}{100}$ = [    ]

**14** 2 tenths 9 hundredths = [    ]

**15** 8 ones and 4 hundredths = [    ]

**Express each decimal as hundredths.**

**16** 0.23 = [    ] hundredths

**17** 4.01 = [    ] hundredths

**Find the missing numbers.**

**18** 67.09 = ⬚ tens 7 ones and ⬚ hundredths

**19** 2.75 = 2 + 0.7 + ⬚

**20** 7.25 = 7 + $\dfrac{⬚}{10}$ + $\dfrac{5}{⬚}$

**Find the missing words or numbers.**

| Tens | Ones | Tenths | Hundredths |
|------|------|--------|------------|
| 8 | 4 • | 2 | 9 |

**21** The digit 8 is in the ⬚ place.

**22** The digit 2 stands for ⬚ .

**23** The value of the digit 9 is ⬚ .

**Express each amount using a dollar sign and decimal point.**

**24** 35¢ = $⬚

**25** 50¢ = $⬚

**26** 9¢ = $⬚

**Write each amount in decimal form.**

**27** 9 dollars and 15 cents = $⬚

**28** 2 dollars and 40 cents = $⬚

**29** 24 dollars = $⬚

**30** 56 dollars and 5 cents = $⬚

ON YOUR OWN

Go to Workbook B:
Practice 2, pages 5–8

# Lesson 7.3 Comparing Decimals

## Lesson Objectives

- Compare and order decimals.
- Complete number patterns.

**Vocabulary**

| more than | least |
|-----------|-------|
| less than | greatest |
| greater than | order |

**Learn Use models to find 0.1 more than or 0.1 less than.**

What is 0.1 **more than** 0.6?

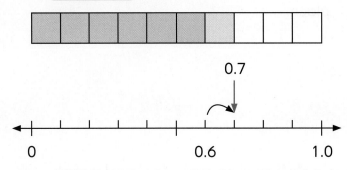

Each part is 0.1.

0.7 is 0.1 more than 0.6.

What is 0.1 **less than** 1.6?

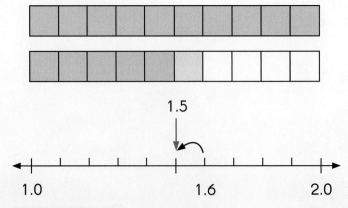

1.5 is 0.1 less than 1.6.

## ᴸᵉᵃʳⁿ **Find 0.01 more than or 0.01 less than.**

What is 0.01 more than 0.22?

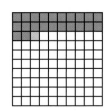 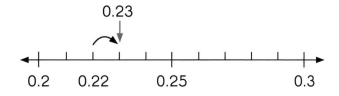

Each part is 0.01.
0.23 is 0.01 more than 0.22.

What is 0.01 less than 0.18?

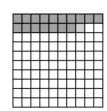 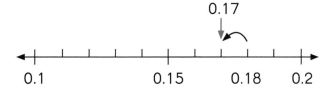

0.17 is 0.01 less than 0.18.

## Guided Learning

**Complete.**

**1** What number is 0.1 more than 1.2? ⬚

**2** What number is 0.1 less than 0.9? ⬚

**3** 0.2 more than 8.7 is ⬚ .

**4** 0.5 less than 4.9 is ⬚ .

**5** What number is 0.01 more than 0.15? ⬚

**6** What number is 0.01 less than 0.29? ⬚

**7** 0.02 more than 6.24 is ⬚ .

**8** 0.04 less than 7.16 is ⬚ .

### Learn **Find missing numbers in a pattern.**

These decimals follow a pattern.
What are the next two decimals?

0.2   0.4   0.6   0.8   1.0 ...

1.2 is 0.2 more than 1.0.
1.4 is 0.2 more than 1.2.

+ 0.2   + 0.2   + 0.2
... 0.4     0.6 ...
Add 0.2 to get
the next number.

The next two decimals are 1.2 and 1.4.

................................................

1.32   1.27   1.22   1.17   1.12

1.07 is 0.05 less than 1.12.
1.02 is 0.05 less than 1.07.

− 0.05   − 0.05   − 0.05
... 1.27     1.22 ...
Subtract 0.05 to get
the next number.

The next two decimals are 1.07 and 1.02.

## Guided Learning

### Find the missing numbers in each pattern.

**9**

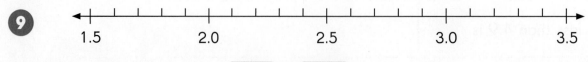

1.5          2.0          2.5          3.0          3.5

1.6   1.9   2.2   2.5   ▢   ▢

**10**

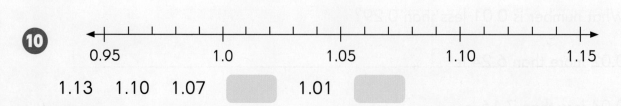

0.95          1.0          1.05          1.10          1.15

1.13   1.10   1.07   ▢   1.01   ▢

# Let's Practice

**Copy the number line. Find each decimal.**
**Then mark ✗ to show where each decimal is located.**

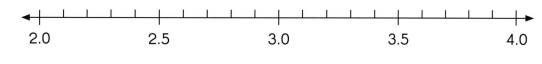

2.0    2.5    3.0    3.5    4.0

**1** 0.1 more than 3.2

**2** 0.1 less than 3.8

**3** 0.2 more than 2.9

**4** 0.3 less than 3.2

**Copy the number line. Find each decimal.**
**Then mark ✗ to show where each decimal is located.**

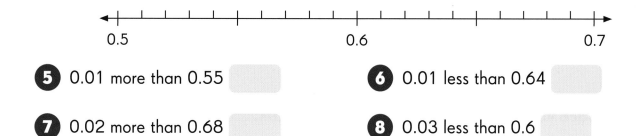

0.5    0.6    0.7

**5** 0.01 more than 0.55

**6** 0.01 less than 0.64

**7** 0.02 more than 0.68

**8** 0.03 less than 0.6

**Find the missing numbers.**

|    | Number | 0.1 More Than the Number | 0.01 More Than the Number |
|----|--------|--------------------------|---------------------------|
| **9**  | 0.19 |  |  |
| **10** | 1.73 |  |  |
| **11** | 3.9  |  |  |

**Find the missing numbers.**

| | Number | 0.1 Less Than the Number | 0.01 Less Than the Number |
|---|---|---|---|
| **12** | 0.28 | | |
| **13** | 3.60 | | |
| **14** | 7.1 | | |

**Find the missing numbers in each pattern.**

**15** 2.2   2.4   2.6   ☐   ☐

**16** 3.34   3.37   ☐   ☐   3.46

**17** 6.23   ☐   6.19   6.17   ☐

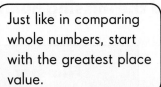

**ON YOUR OWN**

**Go to Workbook B: Practice 3, pages 9–10**

**Learn Use place value concepts to compare decimals.**

Which is greater, 0.4 or 0.34?

| Ones | | Tenths | Hundredths |
|---|---|---|---|
| 0 | • | 4 | |
| 0 | • | 3 | 4 |

First, compare the ones. They are the same.
Next, compare the tenths.
4 tenths is **greater than** 3 tenths.
So, 0.4 is greater than 0.34 and
0.34 is less than 0.4.

greater than: >
less than: <

Just like in comparing whole numbers, start with the greatest place value.

## Learn Use place value concepts to order decimals.

Order 0.62, 0.23, and 0.6 from **least** to **greatest**.

| Ones | Tenths | Hundredths |
|---|---|---|
| 0 . | 6 | 2 |
| 0 . | 2 | 3 |
| 0 . | 6 | 0 |

Remember
0.6 = 0.60.

First, compare the ones. They are the same.
Next, compare the tenths. 6 tenths is greater than 2 tenths.
So, 0.23 is the least.

Because 0.62 and 0.6 have the same tenths digits, compare the hundredths.
2 hundredths is greater than 0 hundredths.
So, 0.62 is greater than 0.6.
The order from least to greatest is 0.23, 0.6, 0.62.

## Guided Learning

### Compare. Use > or <.

11. 0.76 ◯ 0.8
12. 0.4 ◯ 0.24
13. 0.21 ◯ 0.12
14. 0.30 ◯ 0.33

### Order the decimals from least to greatest.

15. 0.18, 0.2, 0.15
16. 0.8, 0.17, 0.31
17. 1.04, 0.04, 0.14
18. 0.20, 2.02, 0.22

You can use place-value charts to help you compare these decimals.

Material:
• 12 cards

# Decimal Game!

**STEP 1** Make a set of cards like these:

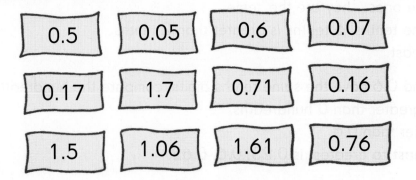

| 0.5 | 0.05 | 0.6 | 0.07 |
| 0.17 | 1.7 | 0.71 | 0.16 |
| 1.5 | 1.06 | 1.61 | 0.76 |

**STEP 2** Shuffle the cards.

**STEP 3** Draw three cards and order the decimals from least to greatest.

**STEP 4** Your partner checks the answer.

**STEP 5** Return the cards to the deck and shuffle them.

**STEP 6** Take turns to order the decimals and check the answer.
Play three rounds each.

The player with the most correct answers wins!

**Hands-On Activity**

Material:
• a ten-sided die

**WORKING TOGETHER**

Work in groups of three.

**STEP 1** Player 1 rolls the die twice to get a 2-digit decimal.
Do not use 0.01 and 0.99.

**STEP 2** Player 2 says a decimal between 0 and 1 that is greater than
Player 1's decimal.

**STEP 3** Player 3 says a decimal between 0 and 1 that is less than
Player 1's decimal.

**STEP 4** Take turns forming a decimal between 0 and 1.
During each round, discuss your answers.

# Let's Explore!

**WORK IN PAIRS**

Your teacher will call out a decimal, such as 2.8.

**STEP 1** Write this number on a place-value chart.

**STEP 2** Insert a zero at any place in this decimal, for example, 2.08. Write this number beneath the first one on the place-value chart.

**STEP 3** Compare the decimal formed with the given decimal. Then say whether it is greater than, less than, or equal to the given decimal.

## Example

| Ones | | Tenths | Hundredths |
|:---:|:---:|:---:|:---:|
| 2 | . | 8 | |
| 2 | . | 0 | 8 |

2.08 is less than 2.8.

**STEP 4** Next, insert the zero in a different place, and write the number on your place-value chart. For example, make 2.80. Then say whether it is greater than, less than, or equal to the given decimal.

Discuss with your classmates how inserting a zero in the different places of a decimal will change its value.

Both Andy and Rita think that 0.23 is greater than 0.3.

23 is greater than 3,
so 0.23 is greater than 0.3.

23 tenths is greater
than 3 tenths, so 0.23
is greater than 0.3.

Do you agree? Why or why not? Explain your answer.

**Compare each pair of decimals. Use > or <.**

**1**

| Ones | | Tenths | Hundredths |
|---|---|---|---|
| 0 | | 7 | 0 |
| 2 | | 7 | 7 |

0.70 ⬤ 2.77

**2**

| Ones | | Tenths | Hundredths |
|---|---|---|---|
| 2 | | 7 | 6 |
| 2 | | 7 | 7 |

2.76 ⬤ 2.77

**Order the decimals from least to greatest.**

**3**  0.49,  0.4,  0.53

**4**  2.8,  2.08,  2.88

**Order the decimals from greatest to least.**

**5**  0.51,  0.57,  1.02

**6**  4.32,  2.43,  3.24

ON YOUR OWN

**Go to Workbook B:**
Practice 4, pages 11–12

# Lesson 7.4 Rounding Decimals

## Lesson Objective

- Round decimals to the nearest whole number or tenth.

**Vocabulary**
round

### Learn Round decimals to the nearest whole number.

The crack in the Liberty Bell is about 24.5 inches long.
**Round** 24.5 inches to the nearest inch.

24.0 ← round down | 24.5 | round up → 25.0

Look at 24.5 on the number line.
It is halfway between 24 and 25.
To round to the nearest whole number, look at the tenths digit.
Since it is 5, round up.
So, 24.5 rounded to the nearest whole number is 25.
The length of the crack in the Liberty Bell to the nearest inch is 25 inches.

Jasmine's mass is 35.2 kilograms.

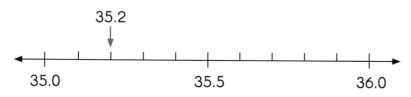

35.2

35.0　　　　35.5　　　　36.0

What is my mass to the nearest kilogram?

The number 35.2 is between 35 and 36.
It is nearer to 35 than to 36.
Since the tenths digit is less than 5, round down.
So, 35.2 rounded to the nearest whole number is 35.
Jasmine's mass to the nearest kilogram is 35 kilograms.

Continued on next page

Round 26.8 to the nearest whole number.

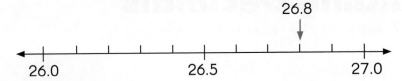

The number 26.8 is between 26 and 27.
It is nearer to 27 than to 26.
Since the tenths digit is greater than 5, round up.
So, 26.8 rounded to the nearest whole number is 27.

Round 14.68 to the nearest whole number.

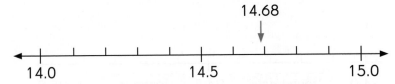

The number 14.68 is between 14 and 15.
It is nearer to 15 than to 14.
Since the tenths digit is greater than 5, round up.
So, 14.68 rounded to the nearest whole number is 15.

Round 39.45 to the nearest whole number.

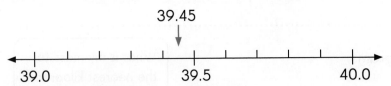

The number 39.45 is between 39 and 40.
It is nearer to 39 than to 40.
Since the tenths digit is less than 5, round down.
So, 39.45 rounded to the nearest whole number is 39.

What would 39.55 be, rounded to the nearest whole number?

## Guided Learning

**For each decimal, draw a number line. Mark X to show where the decimal is located. Then round it to the nearest whole number.**

**Example**

5.8

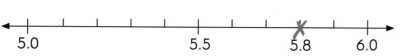

5.8 rounded to the nearest whole number is 6.

**1** 0.7 ⬜   **2** 4.3 ⬜   **3** 0.45 ⬜   **4** 12.53 ⬜

# Let's Practice

**Round the decimals to the nearest whole number.**

**1** Round 3.7 to the nearest whole number.

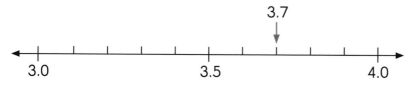

3.7 is between 3 and ⬜ .

3.7 is nearer to ⬜ than to ⬜ .

3.7 rounded to the nearest whole number is ⬜ .

**2** Round 1.84 to the nearest whole number.

1.84 is between 1 and ⬜ .

1.84 is nearer to ⬜ than to ⬜ .

1.84 rounded to the nearest whole number is ⬜ .

**ON YOUR OWN**

**Go to Workbook B:
Practice 5, pages 13–14**

**Round decimals to the nearest tenth.** ——————

Dion's height is 0.83 meter. Round 0.83 meter to the nearest tenth of a meter.

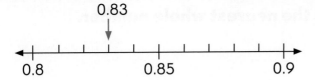

0.83 = 8 tenths 3 hundredths
0.83 is between 8 tenths (0.8) and 9 tenths (0.9).
It is nearer to 0.8 than to 0.9.
To round to the nearest tenth, look at the hundredths digit.
Since it is less than 5, round down.
So, 0.83 meter rounded to the nearest tenth is 0.8 meter.

Round 1.75 to the nearest tenth.

1.75 is halfway between 1.7 and 1.8.
Since the hundredths digit is 5, round up.
So, 1.75 rounded to the nearest tenth is 1.8.

Round 2.98 to the nearest tenth.

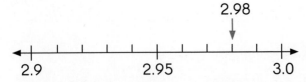

2.98 is between 2.9 and 3.
It is nearer to 3 than to 2.9.
Since the hundredths digit is greater than 5, round up.
So, 2.98 rounded to the nearest tenth is 3.0.
3 is written as 3.0 to one decimal place.

# Guided Learning

**For each decimal, draw a number line. Mark X to show where the decimal is located. Then round it to the nearest tenth.**

**Example**

3.43

So, 3.43 rounded to the nearest tenth is 3.4.

**5** 0.36

**6** 2.32

**7** 4.05

---

 **Hands-On Activity**

Material:
• measuring tape

**WORKING TOGETHER**

Work in groups of four or five.

**STEP 1** Place the measuring tape on the floor, metric side up.

**STEP 2** Each member should take turns to walk 5 steps beside the measuring tape.

**STEP 3** Measure the distance in meters to two decimal places.

**STEP 4** Record the readings in a table.

**STEP 5** Round each distance to the nearest tenth of a meter.

**Example**

| Name of Student | Distance (m) | |
| --- | --- | --- |
| | **Actual Reading** | **Rounded Reading** |
| Eduardo | 1.29 | 1.3 |

**Example**

A number has two decimal places.

It is 1.7 when rounded to the nearest tenth.

What could the number be?

Zach draws a number line to find the number.

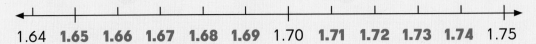

1.64  **1.65  1.66  1.67  1.68  1.69**  1.70  **1.71  1.72  1.73  1.74**  1.75

The numbers in **green** are the possible answers.

A number has two decimal places.
It is 4.2 when rounded to one decimal place.

**1** What could the number be? List the possible answers.

**2** Which of these numbers is the greatest?

**3** Which of these numbers is the least?

# Let's Practice

**Find the missing numbers.**

**1** Round 0.24 to the nearest tenth.

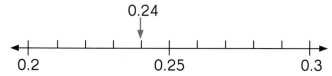

0.24 is between [ ] and [ ] .

0.24 is nearer to [ ] than to [ ] .

0.24 rounded to the nearest tenth is [ ] .

**2** Round 5.17 to the nearest tenth.

5.17 is between [ ] and 5.2.

5.17 is nearer to [ ] than to [ ] .

5.17 rounded to the nearest tenth is [ ] .

**3** Round each decimal to the nearest whole number and the nearest tenth.

| Decimal | Rounded to the Nearest | |
|---------|-----------------|--------|
|         | **Whole Number** | **Tenth** |
| 3.49    |                 |        |
| 4.85    |                 |        |

**ON YOUR OWN**

**Go to Workbook B:**
Practice 6, pages 15–16

# Lesson 7.5 Fractions and Decimals

## Lesson Objective

- Express a fraction as a decimal and a decimal as a fraction.

**Vocabulary**
equivalent fraction

**Learn** **Express fractions as decimals.**

Express the fraction $\frac{1}{5}$ as a decimal.

Look at the bar model and the number line.

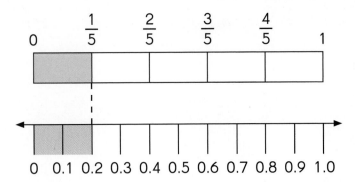

So, $\frac{1}{5}$ is 0.2 as a decimal.

Here is another way to show that $\frac{1}{5} = 0.2$.

$$\frac{1}{5} = \frac{2}{10} = 0.2$$

×2 ×2

Find an **equivalent fraction** with a denominator of 10 or 100.

Fractions show a whole divided into any number of parts. Decimals show a whole divided into 10 or 100 parts.

To express a fraction as a decimal, find an equivalent fraction with a denominator that is 10 or 100.

# Guided Learning

## Complete.

**1**

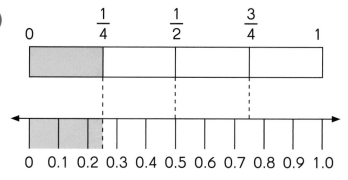

From the bar model and number line, you can see that

$$\frac{1}{4} = 0.25.$$

You can also see that

$$\frac{1}{2} = \boxed{\phantom{xx}} \text{ and } \frac{3}{4} = \boxed{\phantom{xx}}.$$

**2** Express $\frac{1}{4}$ as a decimal.

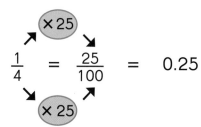

$$\frac{1}{4} = \frac{25}{100} = 0.25$$

Can you find an equivalent fraction of $\frac{1}{4}$ with a denominator of 10?

No. But I can find an equivalent fraction with a denominator of 100.

So, $\frac{1}{4}$ is $\boxed{\phantom{xx}}$ in decimal form.

---

$\mathscr{L}earn$ **Express an improper fraction as a decimal.**

Express $\frac{5}{4}$ as a decimal.

$$\frac{5}{4} = \frac{4}{4} + \frac{1}{4}$$

$$= 1 + \frac{1}{4}$$

$$= 1 + 0.25$$

$$= 1.25$$

$\boxed{\frac{1}{4} = 0.25}$

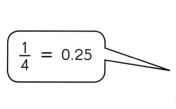

## Guided Learning

**Complete.**

**3** Express $\frac{8}{5}$ as a decimal.

$$\frac{8}{5} = \frac{5}{5} + \frac{\boxed{\phantom{0}}}{5}$$

$$= 1 + \boxed{\phantom{00}}$$

$$= \boxed{\phantom{00}}$$

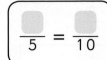 

$$\frac{\boxed{\phantom{0}}}{5} = \frac{\boxed{\phantom{0}}}{10}$$

**Express each fraction as a decimal.**

**4** $\frac{2}{5}$     **5** $\frac{9}{20}$     **6** $\frac{5}{2}$

## Express mixed numbers as decimals.

Express $3\frac{1}{2}$ as a decimal.

**Method 1**

$$3\frac{1}{2} = \frac{7}{2}$$

$$= \frac{7 \times 5}{2 \times 5}$$

$$= \frac{35}{10}$$

$$= 3.5$$

**Method 2**

$$\frac{1}{2} = \frac{5}{10}$$

$$= 0.5$$

$$3\frac{1}{2} = 3 + \frac{1}{2}$$

$$= 3 + 0.5$$

$$= 3.5$$

The whole number 3 remains unchanged. Rewrite the fraction $\frac{1}{2}$ as a decimal.

So, $3\frac{1}{2}$ is 3.5 in decimal form.

## Guided Learning
**Express each mixed number as a decimal.**

**7** $2\frac{3}{5}$     **8** $9\frac{1}{4}$     **9** $5\frac{27}{50}$

**Express decimals as fractions.**

Express 0.8 as a fraction in simplest form.

0   0.1  0.2  0.3  0.4  0.5  0.6  0.7  0.8  0.9  1.0

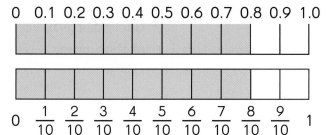

$0 \quad \frac{1}{10} \quad \frac{2}{10} \quad \frac{3}{10} \quad \frac{4}{10} \quad \frac{5}{10} \quad \frac{6}{10} \quad \frac{7}{10} \quad \frac{8}{10} \quad \frac{9}{10} \quad 1$

$0.8 = \frac{8}{10}$

$\quad\quad = \frac{4}{5}$

Divide the numerator and denominator of $\frac{8}{10}$ by 2.

$\frac{8}{10} = \frac{4}{5}$

**Express decimals as mixed numbers.**

Express 2.5 as a mixed number in simplest form.

$2.5 = \frac{25}{10}$

$\quad\quad = \frac{20}{10} + \frac{5}{10}$

$\quad\quad = 2 + \frac{1}{2}$

$\quad\quad = 2\frac{1}{2}$

Divide the numerator and denominator of $\frac{5}{10}$ by 5.

Express 7.25 as a mixed number in simplest form.

$7.25 = 7 + 0.25$

$\quad\quad = 7 + \frac{25}{100}$

$\quad\quad = 7 + \frac{1}{4}$

$\quad\quad = 7\frac{1}{4}$

$\frac{25}{100} = \frac{5}{20} = \frac{1}{4}$

## Guided Learning

**Express each decimal as a fraction or a mixed number in simplest form.**

**10** 0.4

**11** 3.75

**12** 2.45

**Game**

Players: 4 or 5
Materials:
• decimal cards
• fraction cards

# Match Game

**STEP 1** Put all the decimal cards face up on a table.

**STEP 2** Shuffle the fraction cards. Then turn over the fraction card at the top of the stack.

**STEP 3** Check if the fraction on the card shown is equivalent to any of the decimal cards on the table.

> **Example**
> The fraction $\frac{1}{5}$ is equivalent to the decimal 0.2.

**STEP 4** The fastest player to find a match will say 'Decimal snap!' and collect the two cards.

**STEP 5** The other players check the answer. If the answer is wrong, the cards are taken away from the player. The fraction card is put back at the bottom of the stack of fraction cards, and the decimal card is returned to the table.

**STEP 6** Turn over the next fraction card to continue the game.

Play until no more matches can be found.

..................................................
: The player who collects the most matching cards wins! :
..................................................

## Let's Practice

**Draw a bar model and a number line.
Find the missing numbers.**

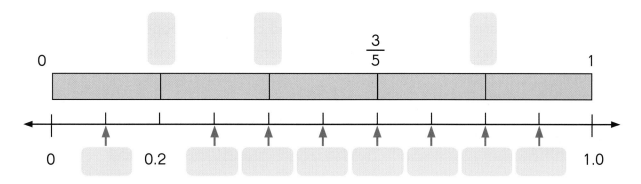

**Use the bar model and number line to express each fraction
as a decimal.**

**1** $\frac{1}{5}$ ⬚

**2** $\frac{3}{5}$ ⬚

**3** $\frac{4}{5}$ ⬚

**Express each fraction as a decimal.**

**4** $\frac{3}{4}$ ⬚

**5** $\frac{17}{20}$ ⬚

**6** $\frac{26}{25}$ ⬚

**Express each mixed number as a decimal.**

**7** $3\frac{13}{50}$ ⬚

**8** $7\frac{24}{25}$ ⬚

**9** $22\frac{4}{5}$ ⬚

**Express each decimal as a fraction or a mixed number in simplest form.**

**10** 0.2 ⬚

**11** 0.75 ⬚

**12** 0.28 ⬚

**13** 3.6 ⬚

**14** 5.12 ⬚

**15** 4.35 ⬚

**ON YOUR OWN**

**Go to Workbook B:
Practice 7, pages 17–18**

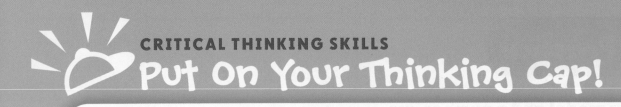

## PROBLEM SOLVING

Suppose this paper strip is 1 unit long. Trace and cut out the paper strip. Use your paper strip to measure these line segments to the nearest tenth of a unit.

**Example**
The line segment is about 0.7 unit.

1

2

3

4

How can you check whether your measurement is accurate?

## CRITICAL THINKING SKILLS
# Put On Your Thinking Cap!

**PROBLEM SOLVING**

Suppose this paper strip is 1 unit long. Trace and cut out the paper strip. Use your paper strip to measure these line segments to the nearest hundredth of a unit.

**Example**

The line segment is about 0.65 unit.

How many tenths are in the paper strip?
How many hundredths are in 1 tenth?

5

6          7

8

**ON YOUR OWN**

**Go to Workbook B:
Put On Your Thinking Cap!
pages 19—20**

# Chapter Wrap Up

## Study Guide

**You have learned...**

**BIG IDEAS**

▶ Decimals are another way to show amounts that are parts of a whole.

▶ A decimal has a decimal point to the right of the ones place and digits to the right of the decimal point.

## Decimals

### Read, Write, and Express in Expanded Form

2.53

- 2 ones and 5 tenths 3 hundredths
- two and fifty-three hundredths
- $2.53 = 2 + 0.5 + 0.03$
- $2.53 = 2 + \frac{5}{10} + \frac{3}{100}$

### Place Value

2 . 5 3

→ 3 hundredths
→ 5 tenths
→ 2 ones

### Patterns

- 1.2   1.3   1.4 ...
  The next number is 1.5.
- 2.28   2.26   2.24 ...
  The next number is 2.22.

### Compare and Order

3.4     3.64     3.46

- $3.46 < 3.64$
- $3.46 > 3.4$
- 3.4 is the least number.
- 3.64 is the greatest number.
- The numbers in order from least to greatest are 3.4, 3.46, 3.64.

### Round to

- the nearest whole number:
  3.6 is about 4.
- the nearest tenth:
  3.62 is about 3.6.

### Fractions and Decimals

- $\frac{9}{10} = 0.9,\ \frac{3}{4} = \frac{75}{100}$
  $\qquad\qquad = 0.75$
- $3.4 = 3\frac{4}{10}$
  $\qquad = 3\frac{2}{5}$

# Chapter Review/Test

## Vocabulary

### Choose the correct word.

| | |
|---|---|
| tenths | least |
| decimal point | greater than |
| decimal form | greatest |
| hundredths | order |
| placeholder zero | round |
| more than | equivalent fraction |
| less than | expanded form |

**1** $\frac{3}{10}$ is written as 0.3 in _____ .

**2** In the decimal 0.43, the digit 3 has a value of 3 _____ .

**3** The decimal 0.44 has a value equal to 4 _____ 4 _____ .

## Concepts and Skills

### Express each fraction as a decimal.

**4** $\frac{3}{10}$ _____

**5** $\frac{23}{10}$ _____

**6** $\frac{127}{100}$ _____

## Express the value of each decimal in ones, tenths, and hundredths.

### Example
2.73 = 2 ones and 7 tenths 3 hundredths

**7** 0.36 _____

**8** 3.07 _____

## 4.12 can be written as $4 + \frac{1}{10} + \frac{2}{100}$. Complete in the same way.

**9** 0.35 = _____ + _____

**10** 1.70 = _____ + _____

**11** 2.04 = _____ + _____

**Continue the pattern.**

**12** 0.2    0.5    0.8    1.1    ⬜

**13** 4.56    4.54    4.52    4.50    ⬜

**Compare. Use > or <.**

**14** 4.1 ⚪ 4.11

**15** 3.02 ⚪ 3.20

**16** 0.6 ⚪ 0.59

**17** 5.87 ⚪ 5.70

**Order the decimals from greatest to least.**

**18** 9.08    9.80    8.09    0.98

**19** 4.62    4.26    6.42    6.24

**Round 9.75 to**

**20** the nearest whole number: ⬜

the nearest tenth: ⬜

**Express each fraction as a decimal.**

**21** $\frac{4}{5}$ ⬜

**22** $\frac{1}{4}$ ⬜

**23** $\frac{5}{2}$ ⬜

**Express each decimal as a fraction or mixed number in simplest form.**

**24** 0.07 ⬜

**25** 0.46 ⬜

**26** 8.75 ⬜

# 8 Adding and Subtracting Decimals

This is Mr. Romero's receipt from a supermarket.

## SUPER SAVE MARKET

| Item | Amount |
|------|--------|
| Broccoli | $3.38 |
| Lettuce | $2.98 |
| Grapefruit | $0.99 |
| Chicken | $6.87 |
| Tomato | $3.18 |
| Grapes | $4.47 |
| Apples | $3.87 |
| **Total** | $25.74 |
| **Cash Payment** | $30.00 |
| **Change** | $4.26 |

*Thank you for shopping at Super Save Market.*

Add to find the total. Subtract to find the amount of change.
$30.00 − $25.74 = $4.26
I received $4.26 change.

## Lessons

**8.1** Adding Decimals

**8.2** Subtracting Decimals

**8.3** Real-World Problems: Decimals

### BIG IDEA

▶ Decimals can be added and subtracted in the same ways as whole numbers.

# Recall Prior Knowledge

## Regrouping ones

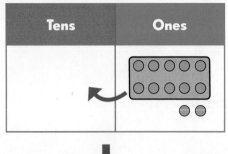

10 ones = 1 ten

12 ones = 1 ten 2 ones
= 12

## Regrouping tenths

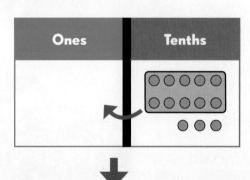

10 tenths = 1 one

13 tenths = 1 one and 3 tenths
= 1.3

## Regrouping hundredths

| Ones | Tenths | Hundredths |
|------|--------|------------|
|      |        | ⊙⊙⊙⊙⊙ ⊙⊙⊙⊙⊙ ⊙⊙⊙⊙ |

10 hundredths = 1 tenth

| Ones | Tenths | Hundredths |
|------|--------|------------|
|      | ⊙      | ⊙⊙⊙⊙ |
| 0    | 1      | 4    |

14 hundredths
= 1 tenth 4 hundredths
= 0.14

## ✔ Quick Check

## Regroup.

**1**

| Tens | Ones |
|------|------|
|      | ⊙⊙⊙⊙⊙ ⊙⊙⊙⊙⊙ ⊙⊙⊙⊙⊙ ⊙ |

16 ones = ☐

**2**

| Ones | Tenths |
|------|--------|
|      | ⊙⊙⊙⊙⊙ ⊙⊙⊙⊙⊙ ⊙⊙⊙⊙⊙ ⊙⊙⊙⊙ |

19 tenths = ☐

**3**

| Ones | Tenths | Hundredths |
|------|--------|------------|
|      |        | ⊙⊙⊙⊙⊙ ⊙⊙⊙⊙⊙ ⊙⊙⊙⊙⊙ ⊙⊙ |

17 hundredths = ☐

# 8.1 Adding Decimals

## Lesson Objective

- Add decimals up to two decimal places.

**Learn** **Add decimals with one decimal place without regrouping.**

Aisha hopped 0.4 meter from the starting line.
From there she hopped another 0.5 meter.
How far did she hop in all?

0.4 + 0.5 = ?

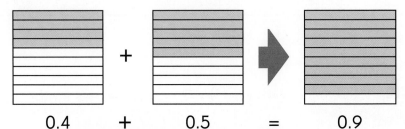

| 0.4 | + | 0.5 | = | 0.9 |

Each square represents 10 tenths or 1.

| Ones | Tenths |
|------|--------|
| 0.4 | ●●●● |
| 0.5 | ●●●●● |

Write the numbers.
Line up the decimal points.
Add the tenths.

```
   0. 4
 + 0. 5
   0. 9
```

4 tenths + 5 tenths = 9 tenths

| Ones | Tenths |
|------|--------|
|      | ●●●●● ●●●● |
| 0 | • 9 |

A decimal in tenths has one decimal place.

So, 0.4 + 0.5 = 0.9.

She hopped 0.9 meter in all.

Add 0.6 and 0.7.

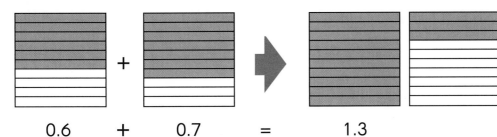

| 0.6 | + | 0.7 | = | 1.3 |

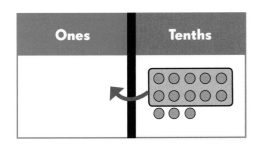

0.6

0.7

Write the numbers.
Line up the decimal points.
Add the tenths.

$$
\begin{array}{r}
\overset{1}{0}.\,6 \\
+\ \ 0.\,7 \\
\hline
1.\,3
\end{array}
$$

6 tenths + 7 tenths = 13 tenths

Regroup the tenths.

13 tenths = 10 tenths + 3 tenths

= 1 one and 3 tenths

So, 0.6 + 0.7 = 1.3.

# Make Wholes

### STEP 1

Player 1 puts his or her 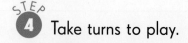 into two groups. Player 1 then counts the 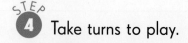 and writes two decimals with one decimal place.

**Materials:**
- 10 decimal squares per player
- some unit cubes per player

**Example**

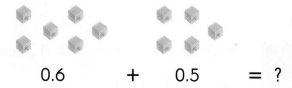

0.6     +     0.5     = ?

### STEP 2

Player 2 adds the decimals by shading the decimal squares.

**Example**

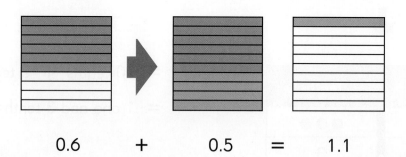

0.6     +     0.5     =     1.1

### STEP 3

Player 2 gets 1 point for shading and saying aloud the answer correctly.

### STEP 4

Take turns to play.

The player with more points after five rounds wins the game!

## Learn

# Add decimals with one decimal place with regrouping in ones and tenths.

Add 5.4 and 7.8.

| Tens | Ones | Tenths |
|------|------|--------|
| 5.4 | ●●●● ● | ●●●● |
| 7.8 | ●●●● ●●● | ●●●● ●●● |

Write the numbers.
Line up the decimal points.

**Step 1**
Add the tenths.

$$\begin{array}{r} \overset{1}{5}.4 \\ +\ 7.8 \\ \hline .2 \end{array}$$

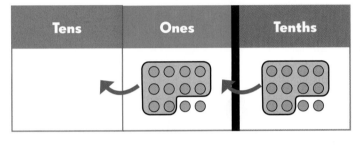

| Tens | Ones | Tenths |
|------|------|--------|
| | ●●●● ●●● | ●●●● ●●● |

4 tenths + 8 tenths

= 12 tenths

= 10 tenths + 2 tenths

= 1 one and 2 tenths

| Tens | Ones | Tenths |
|------|------|--------|
| ● | ●●● | ●● |
| 1 | 3 | 2 |

So, 5.4 + 7.8 = 13.2.

**Step 2**
Add the ones.

$$\begin{array}{r} \overset{1}{5}.4 \\ +\ 7.8 \\ \hline 13.2 \end{array}$$

1 one + 5 ones + 7 ones

= 13 ones

= 10 ones + 3 ones

= 1 ten 3 ones

## Guided Learning

### Regroup.

**1** 16 tenths = [____] one and [____] tenths

**2** 3 tenths + 9 tenths = [____] tenths

= [____] one and [____] tenths

**Add.**

**3**
```
  0 . 4
+ 0 . 2
```

**4**
```
  0 . 5
+ 0 . 6
```

**5**
```
  3 . 5
+ 2 . 9
```

**Copy and write in vertical form. Then add.**

**6** 2.3 + 3.5

**7** 5.9 + 8

**8** 7.6 + 4.8

## Let's Practice

**Add.**

**1**
```
  0 . 3
+ 0 . 4
```

**2**
```
  4 . 5
+ 3 . 2
```

**Complete.**

**3** 18 tenths = [ ] one and [ ] tenths

**4** 6 tenths + 8 tenths = [ ] tenths

= [ ] one and [ ] tenths

**5**
```
  2 . 4
+ 4 . 6
```

**6**
```
  5 . 8
+ 1 . 4
```

**Copy and write in vertical form. Then add.**

**7** 2.6 + 0.7

**8** 1.8 + 2.8

**ON YOUR OWN**

**Go to Workbook B:
Practice 1, pages 21–22**

# Add decimals with two decimal places without regrouping.

Kelvin has 2 pennies. Jasmine has 7 pennies.
How much money do they have altogether?

2 pennies is $0.02.
7 pennies is $0.07.

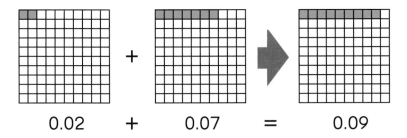

$$0.02 \quad + \quad 0.07 \quad = \quad 0.09$$

| | Ones | | Tenths | Hundredths |
|---|---|---|---|---|
| 0.02 | | | | ○○ |
| 0.07 | | | | ○○○○○ |
| | | | | ○○○ |

Write the numbers.
Line up the decimal points.

| | Ones | | Tenths | Hundredths |
|---|---|---|---|---|
| | | | | ○○○○ |
| | | | | ○○○○ |
| | | | | ○ |
| | 0 | • | 0 | 9 |

Add the hundredths.

$$\begin{array}{r} 0\ .\ 0\ 2 \\ +\ 0\ .\ 0\ 7 \\ \hline 0\ .\ 0\ 9 \end{array}$$

2 hundredths + 7 hundredths
= 9 hundredths

So, $0.02 + $0.07 = $0.09.

They have $0.09 altogether.

A decimal with
hundredths has
two decimal places.

<sup>e</sup>**arn** **Add decimals with two decimal places with regrouping in hundredths.**

Add 0.08 and 0.26.

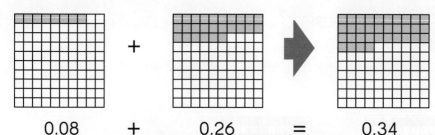

0.08    +    0.26    =    0.34

| | Ones | Tenths | Hundredths |
|---|---|---|---|
| 0.08 | | | ⚪⚪⚪⚪ ⚪⚪⚪⚪ |
| 0.26 | | ⚪⚪ | ⚪⚪⚪⚪ ⚪⚪ |

Write the numbers.
Line up the decimal points.

**Step 1**
Add the hundredths.

$$\begin{array}{r} 0.0\overset{1}{8} \\ +\ 0.26 \\ \hline 4 \end{array}$$

| Ones | Tenths | Hundredths |
|---|---|---|
| | ⚪⚪ | ⚪⚪⚪ ⚪⚪⚪ ⚪⚪⚪ ⚪⚪ |

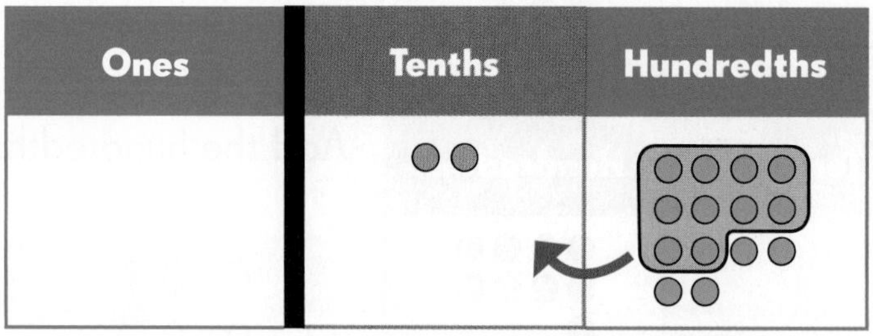

8 hundredths + 6 hundredths
= 14 hundredths
Regroup the hundredths.
14 hundredths
= 10 hundredths +
   4 hundredths
= 1 tenth 4 hundredths

| Ones | Tenths | Hundredths |
|---|---|---|
| | ⚪⚪⚪ | ⚪⚪⚪⚪ |
| 0 | . 3 | 4 |

**Step 2**
Add the tenths.

$$\begin{array}{r} 0.0\overset{1}{8} \\ +\ 0.26 \\ \hline 0.34 \end{array}$$

1 tenth + 0 tenths + 2 tenths
= 3 tenths

So, 0.08 + 0.26 = 0.34.

# <sup>Learn</sup> Add decimals with two decimal places with regrouping in tenths and hundredths.

Add 1.47 and 3.95.

> To add decimals, first write the numbers in vertical form. Make sure you line up the decimal points.

**Step 1**
Add the hundredths.

$$\begin{array}{r} 1.4\overset{1}{7} \\ +\ 3.9\underline{5} \\ \hline 2 \end{array}$$

**Step 2**
Add the tenths.

$$\begin{array}{r} 1.\overset{1}{4}\overset{1}{7} \\ +\ 3.9\ 5 \\ \hline .4\ 2 \end{array}$$

**Step 3**
Add the ones.

$$\begin{array}{r} \overset{1}{1}.\overset{1}{4}\ 7 \\ +\ 3.9\ 5 \\ \hline 5.4\ 2 \end{array}$$

7 hundredths + 5 hundredths

= 12 hundredths

Regroup the hundredths.

12 hundredths

= 10 hundredths + 2 hundredths

= 1 tenth 2 hundredths

1 tenth + 4 tenths

+ 9 tenths = 14 tenths

Regroup the tenths.

14 tenths = 10 tenths

+ 4 tenths

= 1 one 4 tenths

1 one + 1 one

+ 3 ones

= 5 ones

So, 1.47 + 3.95 = 5.42.

## Guided Learning

**Complete.**

**9** 13 hundredths = ⬜ tenth ⬜ hundredths

**10** 7 hundredths + 4 hundredths = ⬜ hundredths

= ⬜ tenth ⬜ hundredth

**Add.**

**11**
$$\begin{array}{r} 0.0\ 8 \\ +\ 0.0\ 4 \\ \hline \end{array}$$

**12**
$$\begin{array}{r} 0.1\ 8 \\ +\ 0.3\ 9 \\ \hline \end{array}$$

**13**
$$\begin{array}{r} 3.4\ 6 \\ +\ 0.7\ 6 \\ \hline \end{array}$$

**Copy and write in vertical form. Then add.**

**14** 4.5 + 6.48 ▢

**15** $10.25 + $6.35 ▢

**16** $1.99 + $1.05 ▢

# Let's Practice

**Add.**

**1**
```
   0.06
 + 0.03
```
▢

**2**
```
   5.63
 + 2.25
```
▢

**Regroup.**

**3** 17 hundredths = ▢ tenth ▢ hundredths

**4** 7 hundredths + 6 hundredths = ▢ hundredths

= ▢ tenth ▢ hundredths

**Add.**

**5**
```
   0.38
 + 0.05
```
▢

**6**
```
   4.4
 + 1.99
```
▢

**7**
```
   2.49
 + 1.86
```
▢

**Copy and write in vertical form. Then add.**

**8** 8.4 + 3.67 ▢

**9** $13.58 + $0.69 ▢

ON YOUR OWN

Go to Workbook B:
Practice 2, pages 23–26

# Lesson 8.2 Subtracting Decimals

## Lesson Objective

- Subtract decimals up to two decimal places.

**Learn** **Subtract decimals with one decimal place without regrouping.**

A bottle has 0.5 liter of water. Abby drinks 0.3 liter of water from it.
How much water is left in the bottle?

0.5 − 0.3 = ?

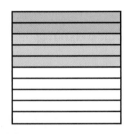

| Ones | Tenths |
|------|--------|

Write the numbers.
Line up the decimal points.
Subtract the tenths.

Take away 3 tenths.

$$\begin{array}{r} 0.5 \\ -\ 0.3 \\ \hline 0.2 \end{array}$$

5 tenths − 3 tenths = 2 tenths

So, 0.5 − 0.3 = 0.2.

0.2 liter of water is left in the bottle.

## Guided Learning

### Subtract.

**1**
$$
\begin{array}{r}
0.9 \\
-\ 0.1 \\
\hline
\end{array}
$$

**2**
$$
\begin{array}{r}
3.5 \\
-\ 1.4 \\
\hline
\end{array}
$$

**3**
$$
\begin{array}{r}
9.9 \\
-\ 0.9 \\
\hline
\end{array}
$$

### Copy and write in vertical form. Then subtract.

**4** 8.9 − 7.8

**5** 7.3 − 4

**6** 9.7 − 2.1

---

**Learn** **Subtract decimals with one decimal place with regrouping in ones and tenths.**

Subtract 0.7 from 1.5.

 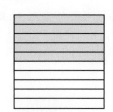

You cannot subtract 7 tenths from 5 tenths. Regroup 1 one and 5 tenths.

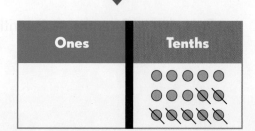

1.5 | Ones | Tenths

1 one and 5 tenths = 15 tenths

Write the numbers.
Line up the decimal points.
Subtract the tenths.

| Ones | Tenths |

$$
\begin{array}{r}
\overset{0}{\cancel{1}}\ \overset{1}{.}5 \\
-\ 0.7 \\
\hline
0.8 \\
\end{array}
$$

So, 1.5 − 0.7 = 0.8.

15 tenths − 7 tenths = 8 tenths

## Guided Learning

### Regroup.

**7** 1 = ▢ tenths

**8** 1.6 = ▢ tenths

**9** 6 = 5 ones and ▢ tenths

**10** 8.7 = 7 ones and ▢ tenths

### Subtract.

**11**
```
    1 . 0
 −  0 . 4
 _____
   ▢
```

**12**
```
    7 . 2
 −  0 . 5
 _____
   ▢
```

### Copy and write in vertical form. Then subtract.

**13** 3.5 − 2.7 ▢

**14** 5.8 − 3.9 ▢

---

**Learn** **Subtract decimals with one decimal place from whole numbers.**

Subtract 0.8 from 2.
You can write 2 as 2.0.
Write the numbers. Line up the decimal points.

**Step 1**
Subtract the tenths.
```
    ¹ ¹
    2 . 0
 −  0 . 8
 _____
      . 2
```

**Step 2**
Subtract the ones.
```
    ¹ ¹
    2 . 0
 −  0 . 8
 _____
    1 . 2
```

You cannot subtract 8 tenths from 0 tenths.
Regroup 2 ones.
2 ones = 1 one and 10 tenths

So, 2.0 − 0.8 = 1.2.

---

## Guided Learning

### Copy and write in vertical form. Then subtract.

**15** 6 − 3.6 ▢

**16** 11 − 3.2 ▢

# Break a Whole!

**Materials:**
- a ten-sided die
- unit cubes
- ten-rods

STEP **1** Each player starts with 1 . It stands for 1 whole.

STEP **2** Player 1 rolls the ten-sided die.

STEP **3** Based on the number rolled, player 1 trades for

and takes away this number of from his or her .

**Example**

STEP **4** Player 1 counts the left and writes a subtraction sentence like this:
1 − 0.4 = 0.6.

STEP **5** Take turns to play.

The first player to take away all the wins the game!

**Subtract decimals with two decimal places with regrouping in tenths and hundredths.**

Subtract 1.06 from 2.24.

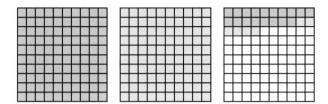

You cannot subtract 6 hundredths from 4 hundredths.
Regroup 2 ones and 2 tenths 4 hundredths.
2 ones and 2 tenths  +  4 hundredths
=  2 ones and 1 tenth  +  14 hundredths

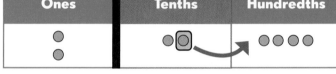

| Ones | Tenths | Hundredths |
|------|--------|------------|

Write the numbers.
Line up the decimal points.

**Step 1**

Subtract the hundredths.

$$2.\overset{1}{2}\,{}^{1}4$$
$$-\ \ 1.0\ \ 6$$
$$\underline{\phantom{2.21}8}$$

14 hundredths  —  6 hundredths
=  8 hundredths

**Step 2**

Subtract the tenths.

$$2.\overset{1}{2}\,{}^{1}4$$
$$-\ \ 1.0\ \ 6$$
$$.1\ \ 8$$

1 tenth  —  0 tenths  =  1 tenth

**Step 3**

Subtract the ones.

$$2.\overset{1}{2}\,{}^{1}4$$
$$-\ \ 1.0\ \ 6$$
$$1.1\ \ 8$$

So, 2.24 − 1.06 = 1.18.

2 ones  —  1 one  =  1 one

## Guided Learning

**Regroup.**

**17** $0.35 = 2$ tenths ▢ hundredths

**18** $1.26 =$ ▢ one and 1 tenth ▢ hundredths

**19** 5 tenths = 4 tenths ▢ hundredths

**Subtract.**

**20**
```
   0.3 6
-  0.1 8
```
▢

**21**
```
   2.3 5
-  1.1 9
```
▢

**22**
```
   6.2 0
-  4.1 8
```
▢

**Copy and write in vertical form. Then subtract.**

**23** $3.85 - 1.69$ ▢

**24** $16.78 - 5.9$ ▢

---

### Learn  Add placeholder zeros to a decimal before subtracting.

Subtract 0.38 from 5.5.
You can write 5.5 as 5.50.
Write the numbers. Line up the decimal points.

**Step 1**
Subtract the hundredths.

```
      4
   5.5 ¹0
-  0.3 8
       2
```

**Step 2**
Subtract the tenths.

```
      4
   5.5 ¹0
-  0.3 8
    .1 2
```

**Step 3**
Subtract the ones.

```
      4
   5.5 ¹0
-  0.3 8
   5.1 2
```

You cannot subtract 8 hundredths from 0 hundredths.
Regroup 5 tenths.
5 tenths = 4 tenths 10 hundredths

So, $5.5 - 0.38 = 5.12$.

## Guided Learning

**Copy and write in vertical form. Then subtract.**

**25** 7.5 − 3.68 [  ]

**26** 2 − 0.55 [  ]

## Let's Practice

**Subtract.**

**1**
```
    0. 8
 −  0. 5
 ───────
```

**2**
```
    0. 0 9
 −  0. 0 3
 ─────────
```

**3**
```
    5. 8 6
 −  2. 1 4
 ─────────
```

**Copy and write in vertical form. Then subtract.**

**4** 7.8 − 3.4 [  ]

**5** $3.94 − $2.71 [  ]

**Subtract.**

**6**
```
    1. 5
 −  0. 8
 ───────
```

**7**
```
    0. 4 2
 −  0. 0 7
 ─────────
```

**8**
```
    2. 4 3
 −  1. 6 5
 ─────────
```

**9**
```
    5. 3
 −  1. 8 6
 ─────────
```

**Copy and write in vertical form. Then subtract.**

**10** 8 − 2.4 [  ]

**11** 24.67 − 8.79 [  ]

**ON YOUR OWN**

**Go to Workbook B:
Practice 3, pages 27–32**

# Lesson 8.3 Real-World Problems: Decimals

## Lesson Objective

- Solve real-world problems involving addition and subtraction of decimals.

**Learn Solve real-world problems.**

Sara has $8.50. She spends $3.75 on a book.
How much money does she have left?

$8.50 − $3.75 = $4.75

She has $4.75 left.

$$\begin{array}{r} \$8.\overset{7}{\cancel{5}}\overset{1}{\cancel{5}}\,{}^{1}0 \\ -\ \ \$3.7\ 5 \\ \hline \$4.7\ 5 \end{array}$$

## Guided Learning

### Solve. Show your work.

**1** For a party, Mrs. Sun buys 2.75 liters of grape juice
and 1.26 liters of apple juice. How much fruit juice does she buy?

[ ] + [ ] = [ ]

$$\begin{array}{r} 2.7\ 5 \\ +\ 1.2\ 6 \\ \hline \phantom{xxx} \end{array}$$

She buys [ ] liters of fruit juice.

earn

# Use bar models to solve real-world problems.

Peter is 0.08 meter taller than Nick. Sulin is 0.16 meter shorter than Peter.
If Sulin is 1.65 meters tall, what is Nick's height?

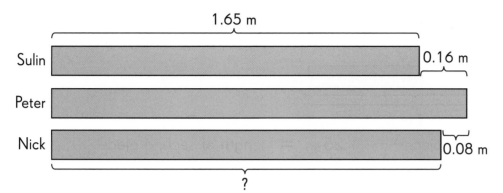

1.65 m

Sulin

0.16 m

Peter

Nick

0.08 m

?

Peter's height  =  Sulin's height  +  0.16 m
$\qquad$ =  1.65  +  0.16
$\qquad$ =  1.81 m
Peter's height is 1.81 meters.

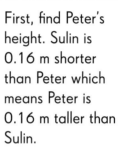

First, find Peter's
height. Sulin is
0.16 m shorter
than Peter which
means Peter is
0.16 m taller than
Sulin.

Nick's height  =  Peter's height  −  0.08 m
$\qquad$ =  1.81  −  0.08
$\qquad$ =  1.73 m
Nick's height is 1.73 meters.

# Guided Learning

## Solve. Show your work.

**2** A pair of pants costs $36.49. A shirt costs $24.95. Victor has $55.00.
How much more money does he need to buy the pair of pants and the shirt?
Cost of pants + cost of shirt  =  total cost

$ [   ]  + $ [   ]  = $ [   ]

The total cost of the pair of pants and the shirt is $ [   ].

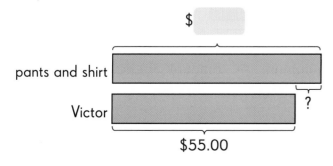

$ [   ]

pants and shirt

Victor                    ?

$55.00

Total cost − $55.00  =  money needed

$ [   ]  − $ [   ]  = $ [   ]

He needs $ [   ] more to buy
the pair of pants and the shirt.

**3** A piece of fabric 4 meters long is cut into two pieces. The first piece is 1.25 meters long. How much longer is the second piece of fabric?

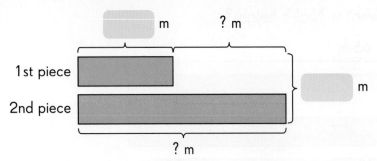

1st piece

2nd piece

? m

Total length of two pieces — 1.25 m = length of second piece

◻ — ◻ = ◻

The length of the second piece is ◻ meters.

Length of second piece — 1.25 m = difference in length between first and second pieces

◻ — ◻ = ◻

The second piece of fabric is ◻ meters longer.

**4** Randy spent \$29.85 on a soccer uniform and \$18.75 on soccer equipment. He paid the cashier \$50. How much change did he get?

\$29.85 + \$18.75 = total cost of uniform and equipment

\$ ◻ + \$ ◻ = \$ ◻

The total cost of the uniform and equipment is \$ ◻ .

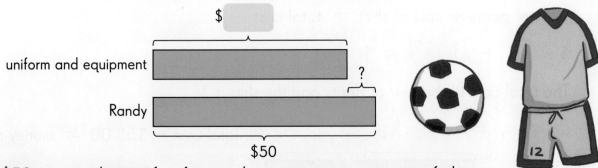

\$50 — total cost of uniform and equipment = amount of change

\$ ◻ — \$ ◻ = \$ ◻

He got \$ ◻ change.

**5** Nathan jogged on Monday and Tuesday. He jogged 4.55 kilometers on Monday and 1.78 kilometers farther on Tuesday than on Monday. What was the distance he jogged on both days?

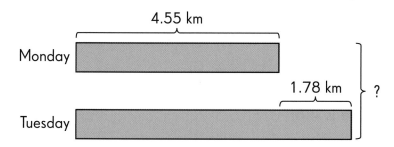

Distance jogged on Monday + 1.78 km = distance jogged on Tuesday

[    ] + [    ] = [    ]

He jogged [    ] kilometers on Tuesday.

4.55 km + distance jogged on Tuesday = distance jogged on both days

[    ] + [    ] = [    ]

He jogged [    ] kilometers on both days.

# Let's Practice

**1** A cup contains 72.85 milliliters of honey. A jar contains 15.2 milliliters more honey than the cup. How much honey does the jar contain? [    ]

**2** Lisa spent $42.15. She spent $15.75 more than Aretha. How much did Aretha spend? [    ]

**3** The weight of a watermelon is 3.6 pounds. A pumpkin is 0.95 pound lighter than the watermelon. What is the total weight of the pumpkin and the watermelon? [    ]

ON YOUR OWN

**Go to Workbook B:**
**Practice 4, pages 33–34**

**PROBLEM SOLVING**

Arrange these numbers in the circles and square so that the sum
of the three numbers along each line is 4.5.

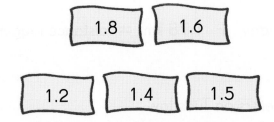

1.8    1.6

1.2    1.4    1.5

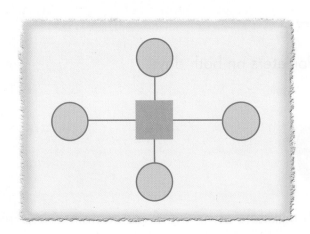

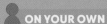
**ON YOUR OWN**

**Go to Workbook B:
Put On Your Thinking Cap!
pages 35—36**

# Chapter Wrap Up

## Study Guide

### You have learned...

**BIG IDEA**

▶ Decimals can be added and subtracted in the same ways as whole numbers.

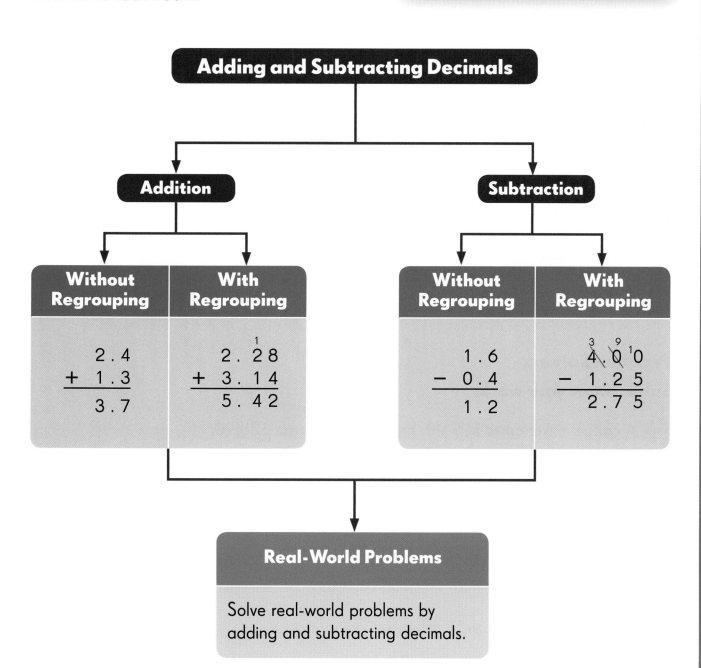

**Adding and Subtracting Decimals**

**Addition**

| Without Regrouping | With Regrouping |
|---|---|
| 2.4<br>+ 1.3<br>——<br>3.7 | 2.28<br>+ 3.14<br>——<br>5.42 |

**Subtraction**

| Without Regrouping | With Regrouping |
|---|---|
| 1.6<br>− 0.4<br>——<br>1.2 | 4.00<br>− 1.25<br>——<br>2.75 |

**Real-World Problems**

Solve real-world problems by adding and subtracting decimals.

# Chapter Review/Test

## Concepts and Skills

### Add.

**1** 3.47 + 6.52 ⬚

**2** 5.04 + 3.62 ⬚

**3** 4.8 + 2.66 ⬚

**4** 7.93 + 4.4 ⬚

**5** 7.05 + 1.98 ⬚

**6** 9.81 + 8.79 ⬚

### Subtract.

**7** 8.64 − 5.01 ⬚

**8** 6.72 − 4.32 ⬚

**9** 6.4 − 4.23 ⬚

**10** 11.5 − 9.45 ⬚

**11** 9.02 − 8.77 ⬚

**12** 30.38 − 12.62 ⬚

## Problem Solving

### Solve. Show your work.

**13** A coffee maker costs $29.90, and a toaster costs $38.90. What is their total cost?

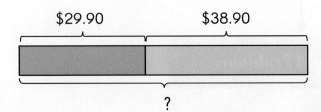

$29.90        $38.90

?

**14** The perimeter of a rectangle is 28.6 centimeters less than the perimeter of a square. If the perimeter of the square is 67.2 centimeters, what is the perimeter of the rectangle?

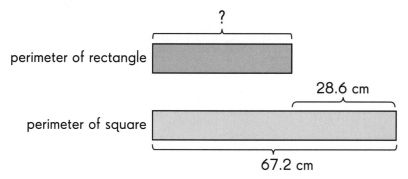

**15** A length of pipe is 3.65 meters long.
Another length of pipe is 1.5 meters longer.
What is the total length of the two pipes?

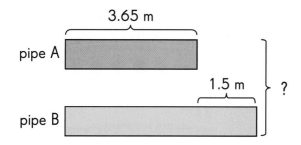

**16** A tank contained 16.55 liters of water, and a jar contained 4.5 liters less. After 3.6 liters were poured out of the jar, how many liters of water were left in it?

# 9 Angles

Scientists have to keep track of the angle of the Leaning Tower of Pisa to make sure that it does not tip over!

## Lessons

**9.1** Understanding and Measuring Angles

**9.2** Drawing Angles to 180°

**9.3** Turns and Angle Measures

## BIG IDEA

▶ Angles can be seen and measured when two rays or sides of a shape meet.

# Recall Prior Knowledge

## Defining a point, a line, and a line segment

| Definition | Example | You Say and Write |
|---|---|---|
| A point is an exact location in space. | • <br> B | Point B |
| A line is a straight path continuing without end in two opposite directions. | C       D | Line CD |
| A line segment is a part of a line with two endpoints. | E       F | Line segment EF |

## Defining angles

An angle is formed by two line segments with a common endpoint.

An angle can also be formed when two sides of a figure meet.

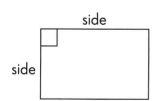

## Making a right angle

Fold a piece of paper like this to get a right-angled corner.

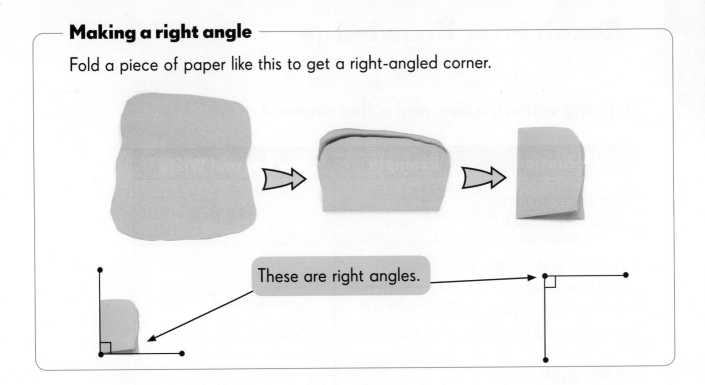

These are right angles.

## Comparing angles with a right angle

Compare an angle with a right angle.

Angle *E* is the same as a right angle.

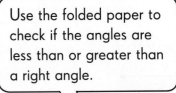

Use the folded paper to check if the angles are less than or greater than a right angle.

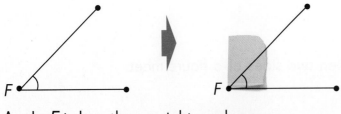

Angle *F* is less than a right angle.

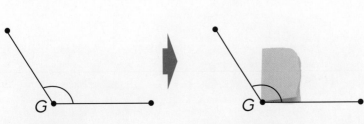

Angle *G* is greater than a right angle.

## Complete with point, line, or line segment.

**1** A _____ is an exact location in space.

**2** A _____ is a part of a line with two endpoints.

**3** A _____ is a straight path continuing without end in two opposite directions.

## Decide whether each figure forms an angle. Explain your answer.

**4**

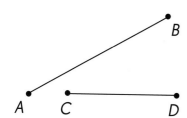

_____

**5**

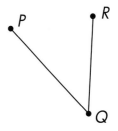

_____

## Name the angle.

**6**

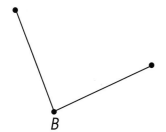

Angle _____

**Copy the shapes. Mark an angle in each shape.**

 **7** Rectangle

 **8** Pentagon

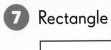

**Decide whether the line segments in each angle form a right angle. Use a piece of folded paper to help you. Explain your answer.**

**9**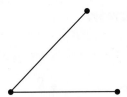

**10**

**11**

**Look at the angles. Then answer the questions. Use a piece of folded paper to help you.**

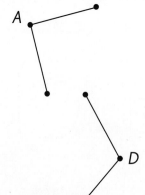

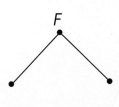

**12** Which angles are right angles?

**13** Which angles measure less than a right angle?

**14** Which angles measure greater than a right angle?

# 9.1 Understanding and Measuring Angles

## Lesson Objectives

- Estimate and measure angles with a protractor.
- Estimate whether the measure of an angle is less than or greater than a right angle (90°).

| | |
|---|---|
| ray | inner scale |
| vertex | outer scale |
| protractor | acute angle |
| degrees | obtuse angle |

**ᴸᵉᵃʳⁿ** **Use letters to name rays and angles.**

A ray is part of a line that continues without end in one direction. It has one endpoint. You can use two letters to name a ray. The first letter is always the endpoint.

$$A \qquad\qquad B$$
ray $AB$

You can write ray $AB$ as $\overrightarrow{AB}$, and ray $BA$ as $\overrightarrow{BA}$.

$$B \qquad\qquad A$$
ray $BA$

In the same way, you can write:

**ⓐ** line $CD$ or $DC$ as $\overleftrightarrow{CD}$ or $\overleftrightarrow{DC}$.

$$C \qquad\qquad D$$

**ⓑ** line segment $EF$ or $FE$ as $\overline{EF}$ or $\overline{FE}$.

$$E \qquad\qquad F$$

$\overrightarrow{PA}$ and $\overrightarrow{PB}$ are rays meeting at point $P$.

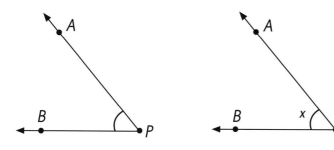

In naming angles using three letters, the vertex is always the middle letter.

The point $P$ is called the **vertex**.
Name the angle at vertex $P$ as $\angle APB$ or $\angle BPA$.
If you label the angle at vertex $P$ as $x$, you can also name it $\angle x$.

**Lesson 9.1** Understanding and Measuring Angles **85**

# Guided Learning

## Name the angles.

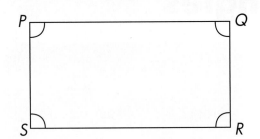

An angle is also formed by two sides of a shape meeting at a point.

**1** Angle at *P*: ∠ ☐

**2** Angle at *Q*: ∠ ☐

**3** Angle at *R*: ∠ ☐

**4** Angle at *S*: ∠ ☐

## Name the angles.

**5**

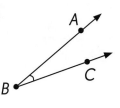

∠ ☐

**6**

∠ ☐

**7**

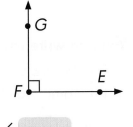

∠ ☐

## Name the angles labeled at the vertices *A*, *B*, *C*, and *D* in another way.

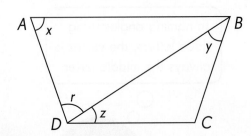

**8** ∠*x*: ∠ ☐

**9** ∠*z*: ∠ ☐

**10** ∠*y*: ∠ ☐

**11** ∠*r*: ∠ ☐

**Hands-On Activity**

Materials:
- two paper strips
- a fastener
- two sheets of drawing paper
- folded paper

**STEP 1**
Paste strip 2 on the drawing paper.
Fasten strip 1 onto strip 2 so that
only strip 1 moves. This is a pair of angle strips.

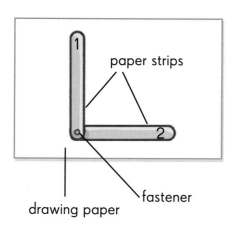

paper strips

fastener

drawing paper

**STEP 2**
Turn strip 1 to make these turns:

- $\frac{1}{4}$ -turn,

- $\frac{1}{2}$ -turn,

- $\frac{3}{4}$ -turn, and

- a full turn.

**Example**

$\frac{1}{4}$ -turn: one right angle

**STEP 3**
Use a piece of folded paper to check
the number of right angles in each turn.

An angle measure is a fraction of a full turn. An angle is measured in degrees. For example, a right angle has a measure of 90 degrees. You can write this as 90°.

You can use a protractor to measure an angle.

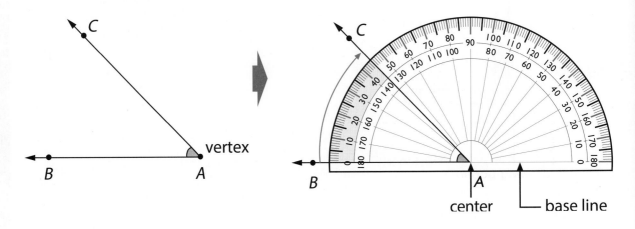

**Step 1** Place the base line of the protractor on $\overrightarrow{AB}$.

**Step 2** Place the center of the base line of the protractor at the vertex of the angle.

**Step 3** Read the **outer scale**. $\overrightarrow{AC}$ passes through the 45° mark. So, the measure of the angle is 45°.

Since $\overrightarrow{AB}$ passes through the zero mark of the outer scale, read the measure on the outer scale.

Measure ∠DEF.

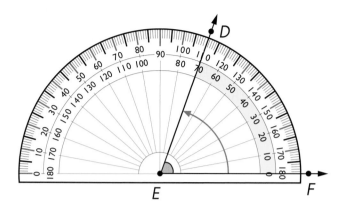

The measure of ∠DEF is less than that of a right angle. It is 70 degrees.

Measure of ∠DEF = [　　] °

Since $\overrightarrow{EF}$ passes through the zero mark of the **inner scale**, read the measure on the inner scale.

## Guided Learning

## Complete.

**12**

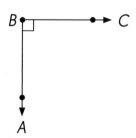

B •——⌐———• → C

A

The measure of ∠ABC is [　] of a turn.

**13**

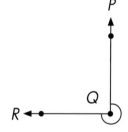

P

Q

R ←•———•

The measure of ∠PQR is [　] of a turn.

**14**   Measure ∠GHK.

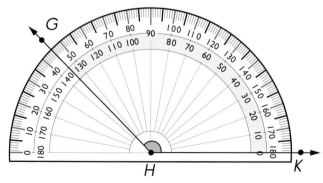

Is the measure of ∠GHK less than or greater than 90°? [　　]

The measure of ∠GHK is [　　] degrees.

Measure of ∠GHK = [　　] °

Explain when to use the inner scale of the protractor.

**15** Measure ∠JKL.

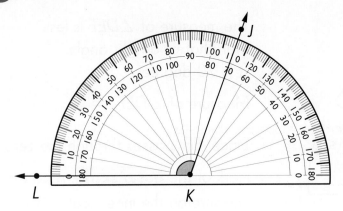

Is the measure of ∠JKL less than or greater than 90°? [ ]

The measure of ∠JKL is [ ] degrees.

Measure of ∠JKL = [ ]°

Did you read the inner or outer scale? Explain your answer.

## Find the measure of each angle.

**16**

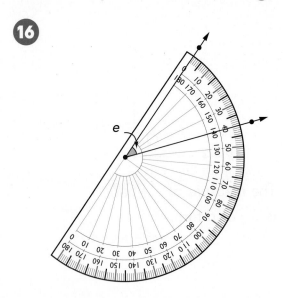

Measure of ∠e = [ ]°

**17**

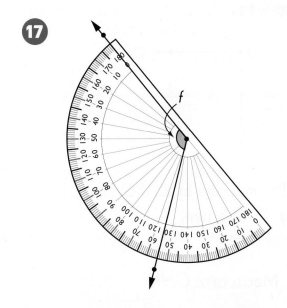

Measure of ∠f = [ ]°

An angle with a measure less than 90° is an **acute angle**.

An angle with a measure greater than 90° but less than 180° is an **obtuse angle**.

So, ∠e is an [ ] angle, and ∠f is an [ ] angle.

## Hands-On Activity

**Material:**
• protractor

**WORK IN PAIRS**

**Estimate the measure of each angle by comparing it to a right angle (90°). Then measure each one with a protractor.**
**Decide if each angle is an acute angle, an obtuse angle, or a right angle.**

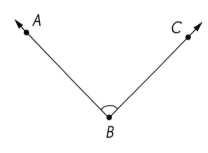

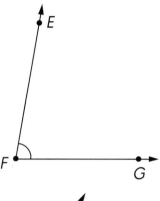

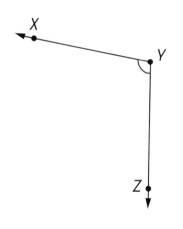

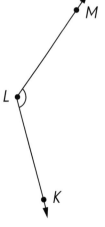

Record your answers in a table like this.

| Angle | Estimated Measure | Actual Measure | Type of Angle |
|-------|-------------------|----------------|---------------|
| ∠ABC | 80° | 90° | Right angle |

**The steps for measuring these angles are not in order.**
**Arrange the steps in order by using 1, 2, or 3 in each box.**

**1** Obtuse angle

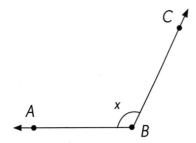

**Step** ☐  Place the center of the base line of the protractor at vertex *B* of the angle.

**Step** ☐  Place the base line of the protractor on ray *BA*.

**Step** ☐  Read the outer scale at the point where ray *BC* crosses it.
The reading is 116°.
So, the angle measure is 116°.

**2** Acute angle

**Step** ☐  Read the inner scale at the point where ray *NM* crosses it.
The reading is 50°.
So, the angle measure is 50°.

**Step** ☐  Place the base line of the protractor on ray *NO*.

**Step** ☐  Place the center of the base line of the protractor at vertex *N* of the angle.

**3** **Compare the measures of the two angles in Exercises 1 and 2.**
**Use < and > in your answers.**

# Let's Practice

## Name and measure the angles.

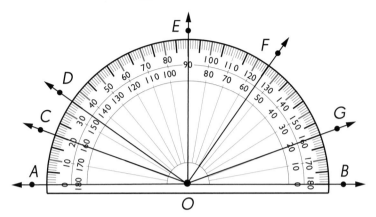

**1** Name two angles that are right angles.

**2** Name four angles that are acute angles.
What are the measures of these angles?

**3** Name four angles that are obtuse angles.
What are the measures of these angles?

## Use a protractor to find the measure of each angle.

**4**

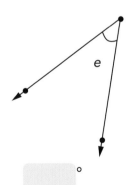

_e_

_____ °

**5**

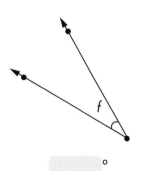

_f_

_____ °

**6**

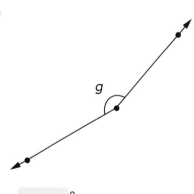

_g_

_____ °

## Use a protractor to measure each marked angle.

**7**

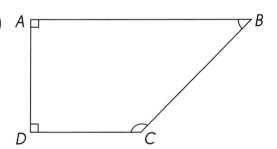

ON YOUR OWN

**Go to Workbook B:**
**Practice 1, pages 45–50**

# 9.2 Drawing Angles to 180°

## Lesson Objective

* Use a protractor to draw acute and obtuse angles.

**Learn**

## Use a protractor to draw **acute** and **obtuse** angles.

Follow these steps to draw an angle of 70°.

**Step 1**  Draw a line and mark a point on the line. This point is the vertex.

vertex

**Step 2**  Place the base line of the protractor on the line and the center of the base line on the vertex.

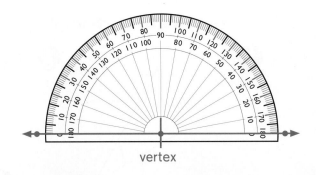

vertex

**Step 3** Use the inner scale or the outer scale to find the 70° mark. Mark it with a dot as shown. Then draw a ray from the vertex through the dot.

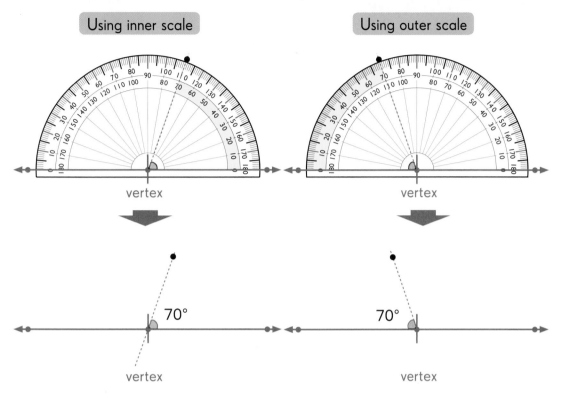

Using inner scale

Using outer scale

vertex

vertex

70°

70°

vertex

vertex

This is how you draw an angle measure of 145°.
Remember to start by lining up the vertex and the base line.

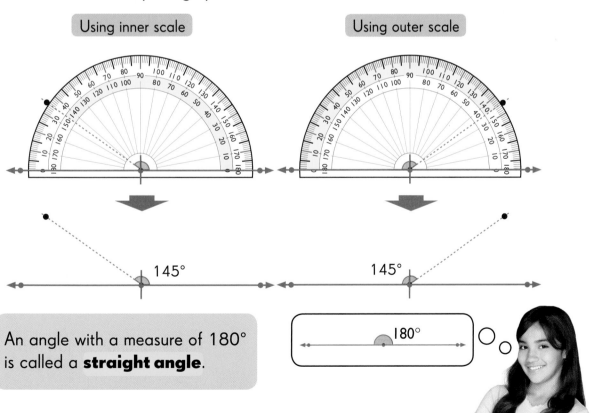

Using inner scale

Using outer scale

145°

145°

An angle with a measure of 180° is called a **straight angle**.

180°

## Hands-On Activity

**WORK IN PAIRS**

Use a protractor to draw angles with
these measures:

**1** greater than 90° but less than 125°.

**2** greater than 10° but less than 25°.

**3** greater than 100° but less than 180°.

**Material:**
• protractor

### Example

An angle measure greater
than 30° but less than 60°.

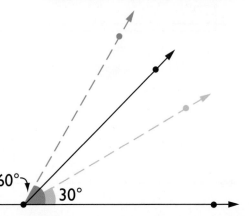

60°  30°

**Learn** **Angles can be drawn in different directions.**

Draw a ray and label it $\overrightarrow{AB}$.
Using point $A$ as the vertex, draw $\angle CAB$ that measures:

**a** 45° so that $\overrightarrow{AC}$ lies above $\overrightarrow{AB}$.

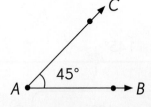

This is an angle above $\overrightarrow{AB}$.

**b** 45° so that $\overrightarrow{AC}$ lies below $\overrightarrow{AB}$.

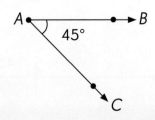

This is an angle below $\overrightarrow{AB}$.

## Guided Learning

**Use a protractor to draw angles.**

Draw a ray and label it $\overrightarrow{QP}$. Using point $Q$ as the vertex, draw $\angle PQR$ that measures:

**1** 55° so that $\overrightarrow{QP}$ lies above $\overrightarrow{QR}$.

**2** 55° so that $\overrightarrow{QP}$ lies below $\overrightarrow{QR}$.

# Let's Practice

**On a copy of these line segments, use a protractor to draw angles.**

**1** On $\overleftrightarrow{AB}$, draw an angle whose measure is greater than 45° but less than 90° at point $C$.

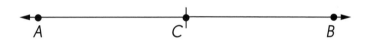

**2** On $\overleftrightarrow{CD}$, draw an angle whose measure is of 125° at point $E$.

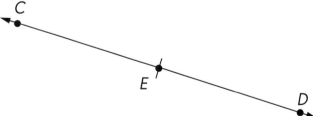

**Complete.**

**3** The measure of $\angle DEF$ is 140°. Draw and label the angle.

**4** Draw:

    **a**    a right angle.

    **b**    an acute angle.

    **c**    an obtuse angle.

ON YOUR OWN

**Go to Workbook B: Practice 2, pages 51–55**

# 9.3 Turns and Angle Measures

## Lesson Objective

- Relate $\frac{1}{4}$ -, $\frac{1}{2}$ -, $\frac{3}{4}$ - and full turns to the number of right angles (90°).
- Understand what an angle measure of 1° represents.
- Find unknown angle measures on a diagram using addition or subtraction.
- Solve real-world problems by finding unknown angle measures.

**Vocabulary**
turn

### Learn Relate turns to right angles.

One right angle

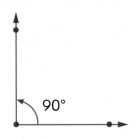

A $\frac{1}{4}$ -turn is a measure of 90°.

Two right angles

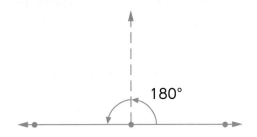

A $\frac{1}{2}$ -turn is a measure of 180°.

Three right angles

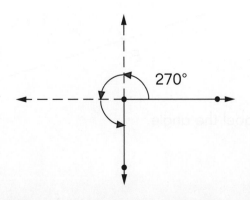

A $\frac{3}{4}$ -turn is a measure of 270°.

Four right angles

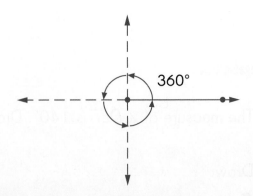

A full turn is a measure of 360°.

 **Hands-On Activity**

Materials:
- paper strips
- fastener
- protractor

 **WORK IN PAIRS**

Refer to the Hands-On Activity on page 80.

**STEP 1** Use a pair of angle strips to make $\frac{1}{4}$-, $\frac{1}{2}$-, $\frac{3}{4}$-, and full turns again.

**STEP 2** On a separate sheet of paper, draw and label the angle formed in each turn in **STEP 1**. Relate each angle to

> An angle measure is a fraction of a full turn. The value is given in degrees.

**a** a fraction of a full turn.

**b** the number of right angles.

**c** Then give its measure.

**Example**

Measure of $\angle d$: $\frac{1}{4}$-turn

one right angle

90°

$d$

**STEP 3** Form and draw an acute angle, an obtuse angle, and a straight angle with your partner. Relate each angle measure to turns using greater than, less than, or the same as.

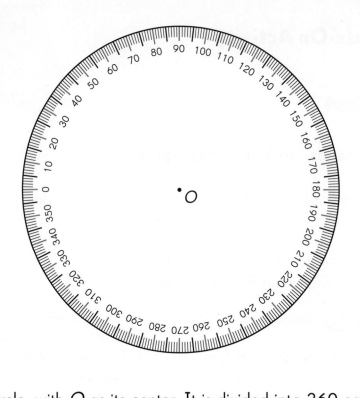

**STEP 4** Use a circle, with *O* as its center. It is divided into 360 equal parts.

**a** Draw a line segment from the center of the circle, point *O*, to the "0" mark on the circle. Label the "0" mark point *A*.

**b** Draw another line segment from the center of the circle to the "1" mark on the circle. Label this point *B*. Use a protractor to measure ∠*AOB*. What is the measure of ∠*AOB*?

**c** What fraction of a full turn is ∠*AOB*? Explain.

**d** When you measure an angle in degrees, what does the number of degrees represent?

## Guided Learning

**1** Complete using $\frac{1}{2}$, $\frac{1}{4}$, $\frac{3}{4}$, or 1.

**a** Two right angles make up a ☐ -turn.

**b** Four right angles is the same as ☐ full turn.

**c** 270° is ☐ of a full turn.

**d** 93° is between a ☐ -turn and a ☐ -turn.

**e** 200° is between a ☐ -turn and a ☐ -turn.

**2** 100° is exactly ☐ of a full turn.

**Learn** **Use a protractor to show angle measures can be added.**

An angle can be divided up into non-overlapping parts.
In the diagram below, $\angle AOC$ is divided up into two
non-overlapping angles, $\angle AOB$ and $\angle BOC$.

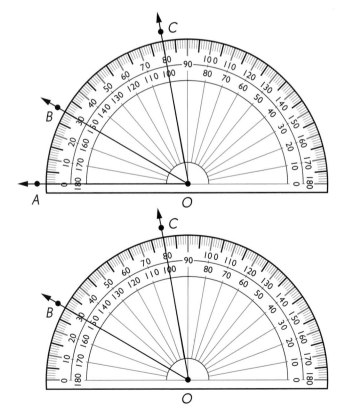

Continued on next page

You can see that the measure of ∠AOB = 30°
and the measure of ∠BOC = 50°.

The measures of ∠AOB + ∠BOC = 30° + 50° = 80°

You can also see that the measure of ∠AOC = 80°.

So, the measure of ∠AOC is the sum of the
measures of ∠AOB and ∠BOC.

You can write the
measure of ∠AOC
as m∠AOC.

## Learn Find the unknown angle measures using addition or subtraction.

ⓐ Find the measure of ∠PXR.

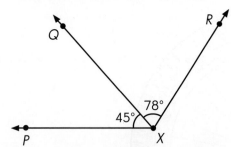

$$m\angle PXR = m\angle PXQ + m\angle QXR$$
$$= 45° + 78°$$
$$= 123°$$

ⓑ The measure of ∠TZV is 98°. Find the angle measure y.

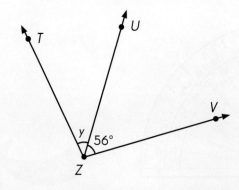

$$\angle y + 56° = 98°$$
$$\text{So, } \angle y = 98° - 56°$$
$$= 42°$$

Jason makes a paper clock for his project. The clock is a circle with three hands showing the hour hand, the minute hand, and the second hand.

**a** Find the measure of ∠AOB.

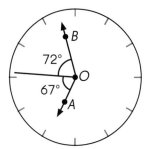

$m\angle AOB = 67° + 72°$
$\qquad = 139°$

**b** Jason then turns the three hands of the clock to form new angles as shown. The measure of ∠COD is 155°. Find the angle measure x.

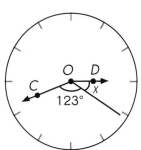

$x = 155° - 123°$
$\quad = 32°$

## Guided Learning

**These figures may not be drawn to scale. Find the unknown angle measures.**

**3**

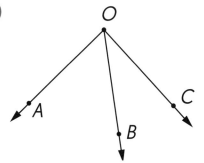

$m\angle AOC = 90°$
$m\angle BOC = 35°$
$m\angle AOB = \boxed{\phantom{000}}°$

**4**

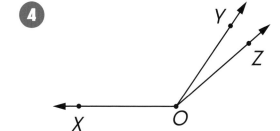

$m\angle XOY = 125°$
$m\angle YOZ = 15°$
$m\angle XOZ = \boxed{\phantom{000}}°$

**5**

*AOB* is a straight line.
$m\angle BOT = 68°$
$m\angle AOT = \boxed{\phantom{000}}°$

**6**

$m\angle FOG = 72°$
$m\angle GOH = 108°$

What can you say about angle *FOH?*

## Let's Practice

**Use the pair of angle strips you made to answer the questions.**

**1** How many turns are in three right angles?

**2** How many turns are in four right angles?

**3** What fraction of a full turn is two right angles?

**Use the pair of angle strips to form these angles.**
**Draw each angle on a piece of paper.**

**4** Angle between a $\frac{3}{4}$ -turn and a full turn.

**5** Angle between a $\frac{1}{2}$ -turn and a full turn.

**6** Angle between a $\frac{1}{4}$ -turn and a $\frac{1}{2}$ -turn.

**These figures may not be drawn to scale. Find the measure of the unknown angle.**

**7** Find the measure of ∠EPG.

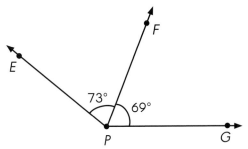

**8** The measure of ∠LQN is 84°. Find the angle measure x.

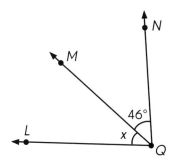

**These figures may not be drawn to scale. Solve. Show your work.**

**9** Sherry buys a paper fan during a carnival.
Find the measure of ∠LTN.

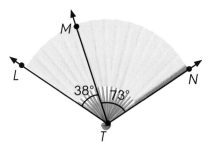

**10** The diagram shows a menu. The measure of ∠XPZ is 168°.
Find the angle measure b.

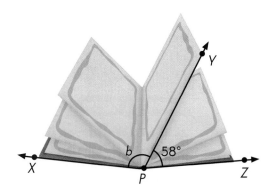

**ON YOUR OWN**

**Go to Workbook B:**
Practice 3, pages 57–63

**PROBLEM SOLVING**

Joshua stands in the center of the circle shown in the picture.

1. If Joshua is facing Blake and he turns around until he is looking at Ian, what fraction of a turn will he make?

2. What angle does Joshua turn through if he moves:

   a.  from looking at Perry to looking at Ian?

   b.  from looking at Roy to looking at Perry?

3. What angle does Joshua turn through if he completes a $\frac{3}{4}$-turn?

**ON YOUR OWN**

**Go to Workbook B:
Put On Your Thinking Cap!
pages 64—65**

# Chapter Wrap Up

## Study Guide

**You have learned...**

**Angles**

**BIG IDEA**

▶ Angles can be seen and measured when two rays or sides of a shape meet.

### Name Angles

Name the angle at vertex $B$ as $\angle ABC$, $\angle CBA$, or $\angle x$.

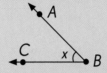

### Measure Acute and Obtuse Angles

An angle measure is a fraction of a full turn. An angle is measured in degrees.

A degree is $\frac{1}{360}$ of a full turn.

The measure of $\angle ABC$ is $\frac{45}{360}$ of a full turn or 45°.

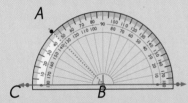

The measure of $\angle DEF$ is 145°.

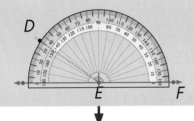

### Adding Angle Measures

The measures of angles that share a side can be added.

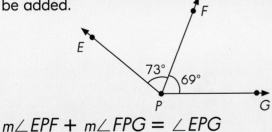

$m\angle EPF + m\angle FPG = \angle EPG$

### Relate Turns and Right Angles

$\frac{1}{4}$ -turn is one right angle or 90°.

90°

$\frac{1}{2}$ -turn is two right angles or 180°.

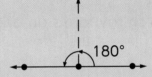

180°

$\frac{3}{4}$ -turn is three right angles or 270°.

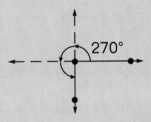

270°

One full turn is four right angles or 360°.

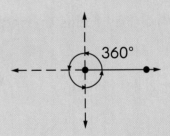

360°

### Solve real-world problems involving angle measures.

# Chapter Review/Test

## Vocabulary

### Choose the correct word.

> | acute angle | protractor |
> | obtuse angle | degrees |
> | straight angle | turn |
> | rays | inner scale |
> | vertex | outer scale |

**1** When two ⬜ meet, they form an angle.

**2** The ⬜ is the point where two rays meet.

**3** Use a ⬜ to measure an angle.

## Concepts and Skills

### Find the correct ray.

**4** Which ray forms an angle measure of 85° with ray *AX*? ⬜

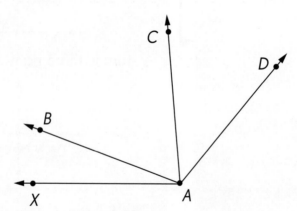

**5** Which ray forms an angle measure of 120° with ray *PQ*? ⬜

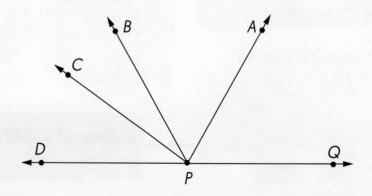

## Draw.

**6** Draw a triangle. Name the vertices of the triangle A, B, and C.
Write x, y, and z inside the triangle so that:

∠x is ∠BAC,
∠y is ∠ACB, and
∠z is ∠ABC.

## Which scale would you use to read the angles shown?
## Use inner scale or outer scale.

**7**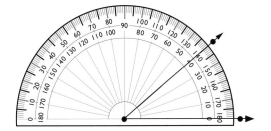

**8**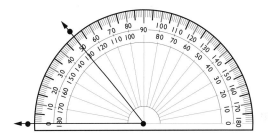

## Use a protractor to measure the angles.
## Then identify the acute angles and obtuse angles.

**9** Angle measure w = [    ] °

**10** Angle measure x = [    ] °

**11** Angle measure y = [    ] °

**12** Angle measure z = [    ] °

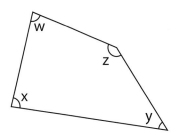

## Draw angles with these measures.

**13** 64°

**14** 170°

## Fill in the blanks.

**15** $\frac{3}{4}$-turn is [    ] °.

**16** 90° is [    ]-turn.

**17** One full turn is [    ] °.

**18** A 30° angle is [    ] of a turn.

**These figures may not be drawn to scale. Find the unknown angle measures.**

 **19**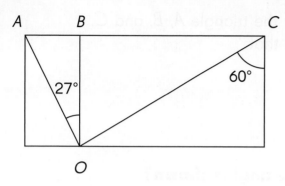

$m\angle AOC = 110°$
$m\angle BOC = $ ____ °

**20**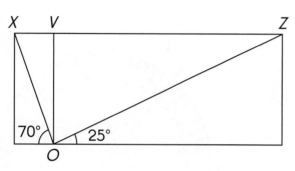

Find $m\angle XOZ$.
$m\angle XOZ = $ ____ °

## Problem Solving

**21** Su Jin folded a paper square in half to form a right triangle, as shown. What is the measure of $\angle BDC$? ____

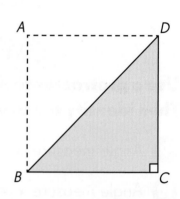

**22** On a clock face, the measure of $\angle AOB$ is shown as 90°. Explain how to find the measure of the other $\angle AOB$. ____

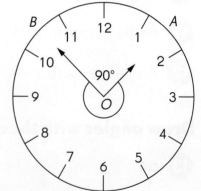

**23** On three copies of this clock face, use the center as the common point and draw 5 angles

**a** which are right angles.

**b** which are 180°.

**c** which are 270°.

# Perpendicular and Parallel Line Segments

The yellow bars are horizontal. The yellow bar above me and the blue post on my right are perpendicular to each other.

The blue posts are vertical.

The bench is horizontal and parallel to the ground. The four blue posts at the corners of the bench are vertical and perpendicular to the ground.

Can he do 30 sit-ups?

**Lessons**

**BIG IDEA**

▶ Line segments can go up and down, from side to side, and in every direction.

## Checking perpendicular lines

Perpendicular lines are two lines that meet at a right angle or 90°.

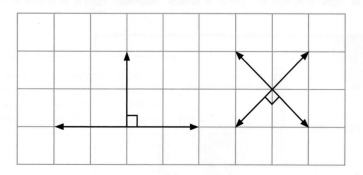

Use a folded sheet of paper or a ruler to check whether two lines are perpendicular.

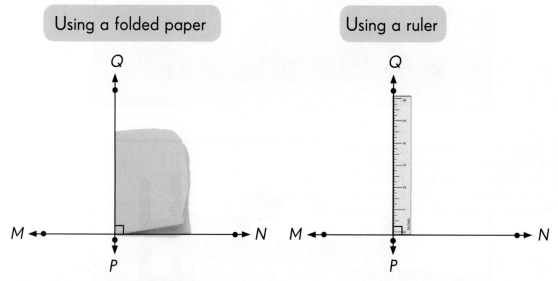

Using a folded paper

Using a ruler

Line *PQ* is perpendicular to line *MN*.

## Checking parallel lines

Parallel lines are a set of lines that will never meet no matter how long they are drawn. They are always the same distance apart.

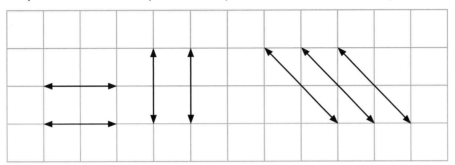

## Finding perpendicular lines in everyday objects

These are perpendicular line segments in everyday objects.

## Finding parallel lines in everyday objects

These are parallel lines in everyday objects.

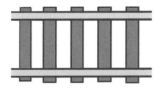 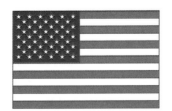 

## Copying perpendicular lines on grid paper

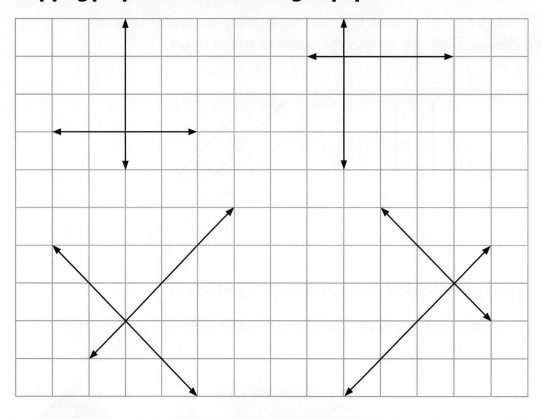

## Copying parallel lines on grid paper

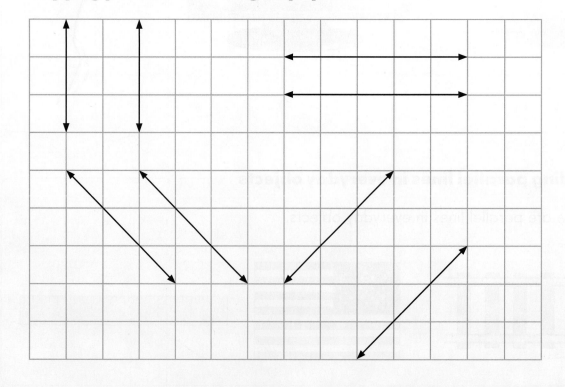

**Which pairs of line segments are perpendicular?**
**Use a folded sheet of paper or straightedge to check.**

**1**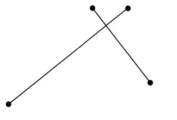

**2**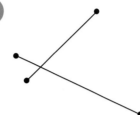

**3**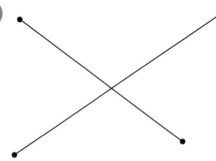

**4**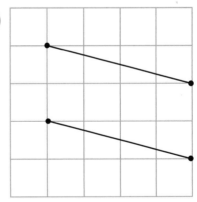

**Which pairs of line segments are parallel?**

**5**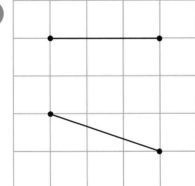

**6**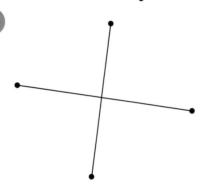

**7**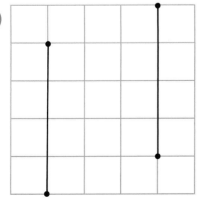

**8**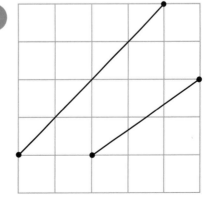

## Complete with perpendicular or parallel.

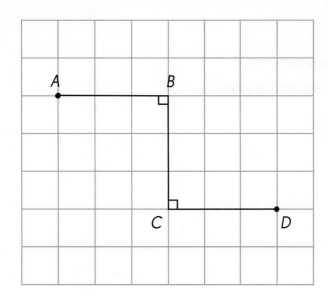

9. $\overline{AB}$ is [ ] to $\overline{CD}$.

10. $\overline{AB}$ is [ ] to $\overline{BC}$.

11. $\overline{BC}$ is [ ] to $\overline{CD}$.

## Name a pair of perpendicular line segments and a pair of parallel line segments.

12.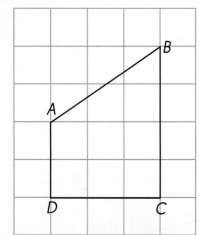

13.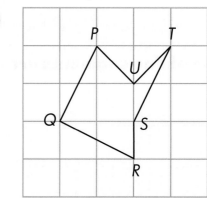

## Identify the perpendicular line segments and the parallel line segments on this picture frame.

14.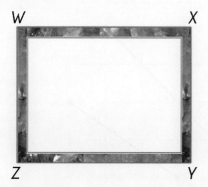

# Drawing Perpendicular Line Segments

## Lesson Objective

- Draw perpendicular line segments.

**Vocabulary**

perpendicular line segments (⊥)

drawing triangle

right triangle

**Learn** **Use a protractor to draw a line segment perpendicular to segment _AB_.**

**Step 1** Mark a point on $\overline{AB}$ and label it _C_.

Place the base line of the protractor on $\overline{AB}$.

Align the center of the base line with point _C_.

Use the inner or outer scale to find the 90° mark.

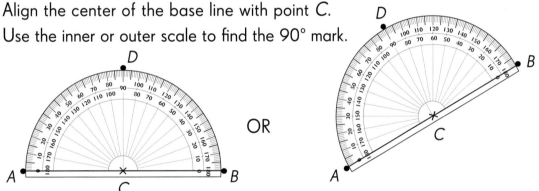

OR

**Step 2** Use a straightedge to connect point _C_ and point _D_.

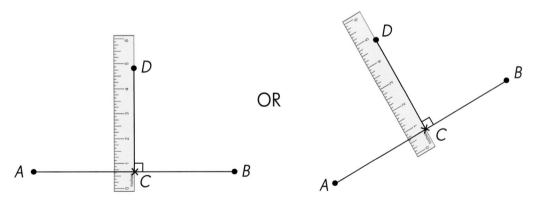

OR

$\overline{AB}$ and $\overline{CD}$ are **perpendicular line segments**.

You can write this as $\overline{AB} \perp \overline{CD}$.

**Use a drawing triangle to draw a line segment perpendicular to segment *AB*.**

**Step 1** Mark a point *C* on $\overline{AB}$. Place the straightedge of the drawing triangle on $\overline{AB}$. Place its right-angled corner at point *C*. Mark a point at the third corner of the drawing triangle. Label this point *D*.

A drawing triangle is in the shape of a **right triangle**, because it has one right angle.

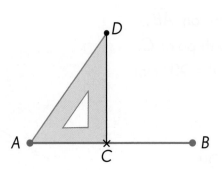

OR

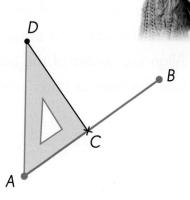

**Step 2** Connect point *C* and point *D*.

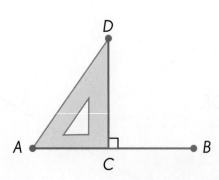

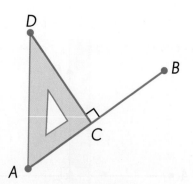

$\overline{AB}$ and $\overline{CD}$ are perpendicular line segments.
$\overline{AB} \perp \overline{CD}$

 **Hands-On Activity**

Materials:
• straightedge
• grid paper

**WORK IN PAIRS**

1. Use a straightedge to draw a line segment. Ask your partner to draw a line segment perpendicular to yours. Reverse roles and repeat.

2. Use grid paper as shown. Draw a line segment perpendicular to $\overline{AB}$ and $\overline{CD}$ without using a protractor. Explain how you drew the line segments.

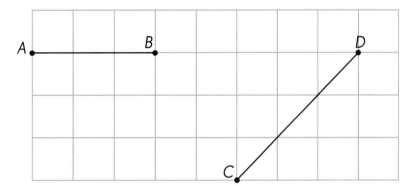

## Guided Learning

**Copy the line segments. Draw a line segment perpendicular to the given line segment through points A and B.**

1.

2.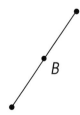

**Copy the line segments. Draw a line segment perpendicular to the given line segment.**

3.

4.

**Look at the figure.**

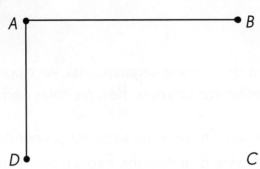

1 Copy the figure. Draw a line segment perpendicular to $\overline{AB}$ and passing through point *B*.

2 Draw a line segment perpendicular to $\overline{AD}$ and passing through point *D*.

3 Extend each line segment you drew in Exercises 1 and 2 until they meet. Label this point *C*.

4 What do you notice about the two line segments you have drawn? What shape did you form?

5 Draw segment *AC*. Name the two right triangles that are formed.

**Complete the figure.**

6 Figure A is made up of two identical squares. Copy and complete the figure on the right to form a figure identical to figure A.

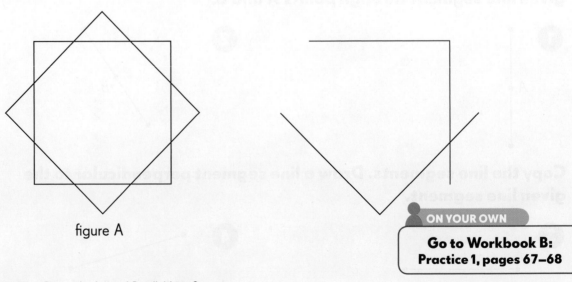

figure A

**ON YOUR OWN**

**Go to Workbook B: Practice 1, pages 67–68**

# 10.2 Drawing Parallel Line Segments

## Lesson Objective

- Draw parallel line segments.

### Learn **Draw a line segment parallel to segment _PQ_.**

**Step 1** Place a drawing triangle against $\overline{PQ}$.

Then place a straightedge at the **base** of the drawing triangle.

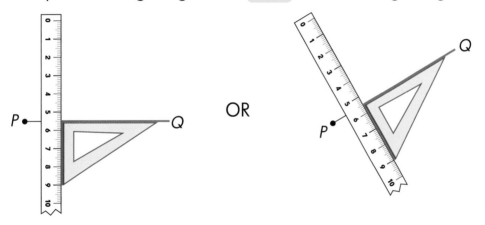

OR

**Step 2** Slide the drawing triangle along the straightedge.

Then use the edge of the drawing triangle to draw $\overline{MN}$.

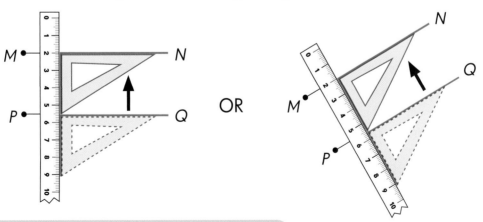

OR

$\overline{PQ}$ and $\overline{MN}$ are **parallel line segments**.

You can write this as $\overline{PQ}$ || $\overline{MN}$.

Draw a line segment parallel to $\overline{CD}$ through point $R$.

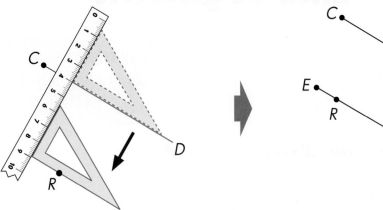

$\overline{EF}$ is parallel to $\overline{CD}$.

$\overline{EF} \parallel \overline{CD}$

Slide the drawing triangle along the straightedge until the edge of the drawing triangle touches point $R$. Then draw a line through point $R$.

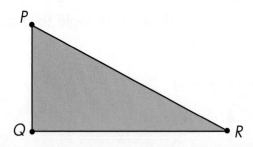

## Guided Learning

**Copy △PQR on a sheet of paper. Then follow the directions.**

P

Q          R

Use a drawing triangle and a straightedge to draw

**1** a line segment parallel to $\overline{QR}$ through point $P$.

**2** a line segment parallel to $\overline{PQ}$ through point $R$.

**3** Extend each line segment you drew in Exercises 1 and 2 until they meet. What do you notice about the two line segments you have drawn?

**4** What do you notice about the figure you have drawn?

 **Hands-On Activity**

 **WORK IN PAIRS**

Materials:
- straightedge
- drawing triangle

**1** Use a straightedge to draw a line segment.
Ask your partner to draw a line segment parallel to yours.
Reverse roles and repeat.

**2** Use a straightedge to draw a line segment.
Then mark a point near it.
Ask your partner to draw a line segment parallel to
the first line segment through the point. Reverse roles and repeat.

**3** On a sheet of paper, copy $\overline{EF}$ and the dots as shown.
Draw line segments parallel to $\overline{EF}$. Each line segment
you draw should pass through one of the given points.

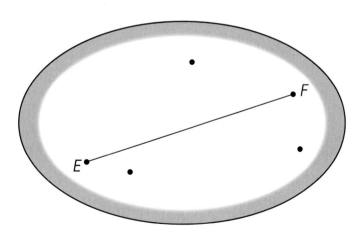

**Complete using a copy of each figure.**

**1** Use a drawing triangle and a straightedge to draw a line segment parallel to $\overline{TU}$ through point $V$.

**2** Use a drawing triangle and a straightedge to draw a line segment parallel to $\overline{AB}$ through point $C$.

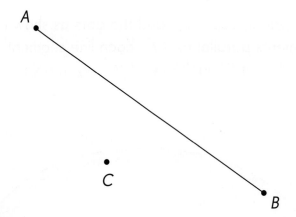

**Complete the pattern.**

**3** Copy the figure. Draw parallel line segments to complete the figure. Color the correct rungs to complete the figure.

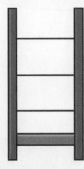

ON YOUR OWN

**Go to Workbook B:
Practice 2, pages 69–70**

# 10.3 Horizontal and Vertical Lines

## Lesson Objective

- Identify horizontal and vertical lines.

**Vocabulary**
horizontal lines
vertical lines

### Learn **Identify horizontal and vertical lines.**

Two pairs of parallel lines are drawn on a sheet of paper and pinned on a wall.

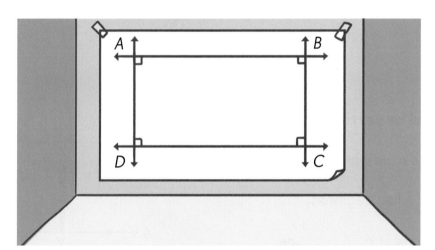

A vertical line is always perpendicular to a horizontal line.

You can write lines $AB$ and $DC$ as $\overleftrightarrow{AB}$ and $\overleftrightarrow{DC}$.

$\overleftrightarrow{AB}$ and $\overleftrightarrow{DC}$ are parallel to the floor.

Both $\overleftrightarrow{AB}$ and $\overleftrightarrow{DC}$ are **horizontal lines**.

$\overleftrightarrow{AD}$ and $\overleftrightarrow{BC}$ meet the horizontal lines $AB$ and $DC$ at right angles.

Both $\overleftrightarrow{AD}$ and $\overleftrightarrow{BC}$ are **vertical lines**.

## Guided Learning

**Look at the picture below. Find the vertical and horizontal line segments. Describe these line segments using the terms vertical, horizontal, parallel, and perpendicular.**

 **1**

**Complete with horizontal or vertical.**

**2** Angela placed a stick *XY* upright on the ground.

The stick *XY* is a [ ] line segment.

The line *AB* on the ground is a [ ] line.

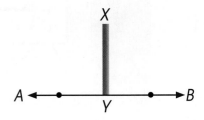

**The picture shows a container of water on a table. Name all the line segments that are described.**

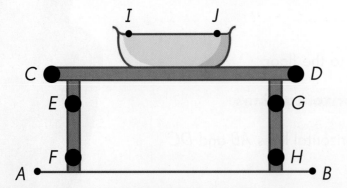

**3** Horizontal line segments: [ ]

**4** Vertical line segments: [ ]

## Look at each picture.

**1** Identify the vertical line segments.

**2** Identify the horizontal line segments.

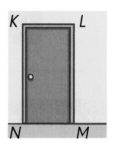

**ON YOUR OWN**

**Go to Workbook B:**
**Practice 3, pages 71–74**

## CRITICAL THINKING SKILLS

# Put On Your Thinking Cap!

**PROBLEM SOLVING**

$X$ is a point not on $\overline{AB}$.

• X

A •————————————————————————• B

Use a protractor, a
drawing triangle, and
a straightedge.

**STEP 1** Copy $\overline{AB}$ and point $X$ on a piece of paper.

**STEP 2** Draw a line segment perpendicular
to $\overline{AB}$ through point $X$.

**STEP 3** Draw two more line segments
to make a rectangle.

**ON YOUR OWN**

**Go to Workbook B:**
**Put On Your Thinking Cap!**
**pages 75–78**

# Chapter Wrap Up

## Study Guide

**You have learned...**

## Lines and Line Segments

### Perpendicular and Parallel Line Segments

Draw a line segment perpendicular to a given line segment
- through a point on the given line segment (use a drawing triangle and protractor).
- through a point not on the given line segment (use a drawing triangle).

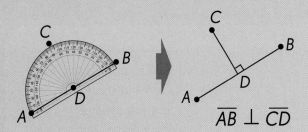

$\overline{AB} \perp \overline{CD}$

Draw a line segment parallel to
- a given line segment.
- a given line segment and passing through a given point.

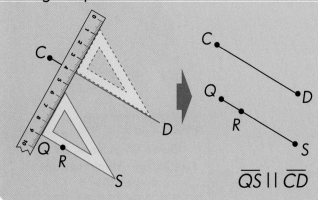

$\overline{QS} \parallel \overline{CD}$

### Horizontal and Vertical Lines

Understand the terms horizontal and vertical lines.
Know that
- all lines parallel to level ground are horizontal.
- all lines perpendicular to level ground are vertical.

Identify horizontal and vertical lines in given figures and in your surroundings.

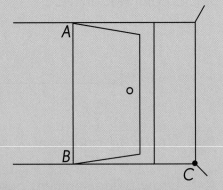

$\overline{BC}$ is a horizontal line segment.

$\overline{AB}$ is a vertical line segment.

# Chapter Review/Test

## Vocabulary

### Choose the correct word.

> perpendicular
> parallel
> base
> drawing triangle
> right triangle
> vertical
> horizontal

**1** When two line segments meet at right angles, they are [　　] to each other.

**2** Two [　　] line segments are parts of lines that are the same distance apart.

**3** A line segment perpendicular to level ground is a [　　] line segment.

**4** A line segment parallel to level ground is a [　　] line segment.

## Concepts and Skills

### Complete with yes or no.

**5** $\overline{PQ}$ is perpendicular to $\overline{RS}$.

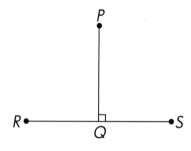

If $\overline{PQ}$ is vertical, must $\overline{RS}$ be horizontal? [　　]

**6** $\overline{AB}$ is perpendicular to $\overline{BC}$.

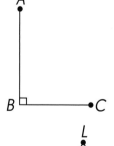

If $\overline{BC}$ is horizontal, must $\overline{AB}$ be vertical? [　　]

**7** Is *LMN* a right triangle? [　　]

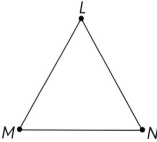

# Copy the line segments.

**8** Draw a line segment perpendicular to $\overline{XY}$ through point $Y$.

**9** Draw a line segment perpendicular to $\overline{PQ}$ through point $O$.

**10** Draw a line segment parallel to $\overline{AB}$.

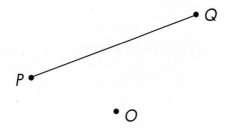

**11** Draw a line segment parallel to $\overline{QR}$ through point $P$.

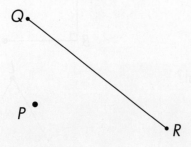

# 11 Squares and Rectangles

What objects are square or rectangular in shape?

**Lessons**

**BIG IDEA**

▶ Squares and rectangles are four-sided figures with special properties.

## Identifying squares and rectangles

square and
rectangle

rectangle

rectangle

square and
rectangle

Rectangles
- Opposite sides are parallel, and are of the same length.
- All angles measure 90°.
- A rectangle may or may not be a square.

Squares
- All sides are of the same length.
- Opposite sides are parallel.
- All angles measure 90°.
- A square is a special type of rectangle.

## Breaking up shapes made up of squares and rectangles

## Finding the perimeter of a square and a rectangle

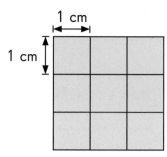

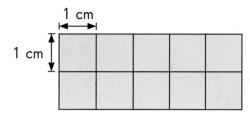

The perimeter of a figure is the distance around it.
So, the perimeter of the square is 12 centimeters.
The perimeter of the rectangle is 14 centimeters.

✔ **Quick Check**

## Identify the squares and rectangles.

1

2

3

4

## Break up each shape into squares and rectangles in two ways.

5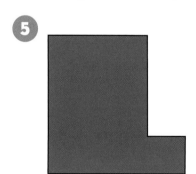

6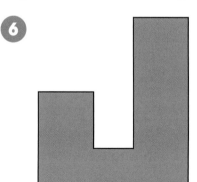

7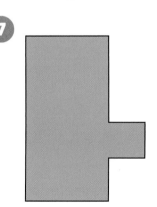

## Complete.

**8** Figure *ABCD* is a square.

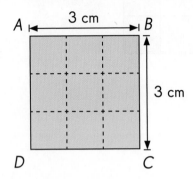

It has four sides of the same length. ⬚ = ⬚ = ⬚ = ⬚

Its opposite sides are parallel. ⬚ || ⬚ and ⬚ || ⬚

It has four right angles. Each angle measures ⬚°.

The perimeter of figure *ABCD* is ⬚ centimeters.

**9** Figure *EFGH* is a rectangle.

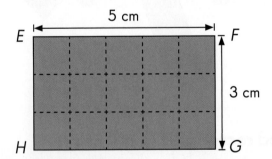

It has four sides.
Its opposite sides are parallel, and are of the same length.

⬚ = ⬚ and ⬚ = ⬚

⬚ || ⬚ and ⬚ || ⬚

It has ⬚ right angles. Each angle measures 90°.

The perimeter of figure *EFGH* is ⬚ centimeters.

# 11.1 Squares and Rectangles

## Lesson Objective

- Understand and apply the properties of squares and rectangles.

**Learn** **Identify a square and its properties.**

This is a square.

A square is a four-sided figure.
It has four sides of the same length.
$AB = BC = CD = DA$

 The tick marks show that the lengths of all sides are equal.

Its opposite sides are **parallel**.
So, a square has two pairs of parallel sides.
$\overline{AB} \parallel \overline{DC}$ and $\overline{AD} \parallel \overline{BC}$

It has four **right angles**.
Measure of $\angle a$ = measure of $\angle b$
= measure of $\angle c$ = measure of $\angle d$
= $90°$

In figure ABCD, the length of each side is 15 inches.

This is a rectangle.

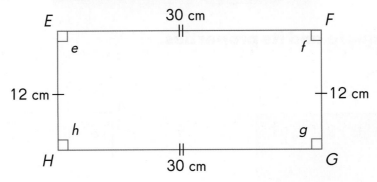

A rectangle is a four-sided figure.

Its opposite sides are of equal length.
$EF = HG$ and $EH = FG$

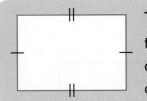

The tick marks show that the lengths of opposite sides are equal.

In figure *EFGH*, the length of $\overline{EF}$ and $\overline{GH}$ is 30 centimeters. The length of $\overline{EH}$ and $\overline{FG}$ is 12 centimeters.

Its opposite sides are parallel.
So, a rectangle has two pairs of parallel sides.
$\overline{EF} \parallel \overline{HG}$ and $\overline{EH} \parallel \overline{FG}$

It has four right angles.
Measure of $\angle e$ = measure of $\angle f$
= measure of $\angle g$ = measure of $\angle h$
= 90°

## Guided Learning

**Look at the figures on the grid.**

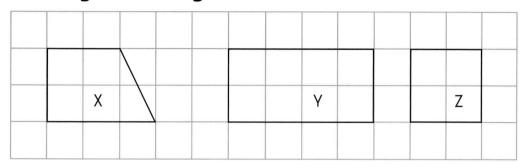

**Check (✓) the boxes to show the properties of each figure on the grid.**

| Property | Figure | | |
|---|:---:|:---:|:---:|
| | **X** | **Y** | **Z** |
| **1** Has four sides | ✓ | ✓ | ✓ |
| **2** All sides are of equal length | | | |
| **3** Opposite sides are of equal length | | | |
| **4** Has exactly one pair of parallel sides | | | |
| **5** Has exactly two pairs of parallel sides | | | |
| **6** Has exactly four right angles | | | |
| **7** Has exactly two right angles | | | |

**Use the properties in Exercises 1 to 7 to identify the figures on the grid.**

**8** Figure _____ is a rectangle and a square.

**9** Figure _____ is a rectangle but not a square.

**10** Figure _____ is not a square or a rectangle.

**Tell which figure is a square. Explain how to identify a square.**

**11**

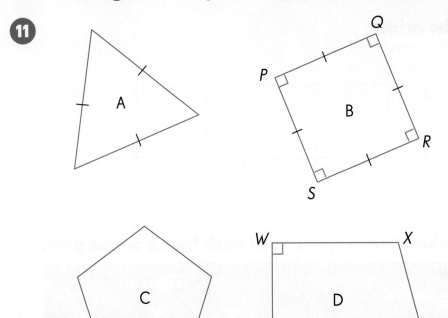

**12** **Which figure, if any, in exercise 11 is a right triangle? Explain.**

**Tell which figure is a rectangle. Explain how to identify a rectangle.**

**13**

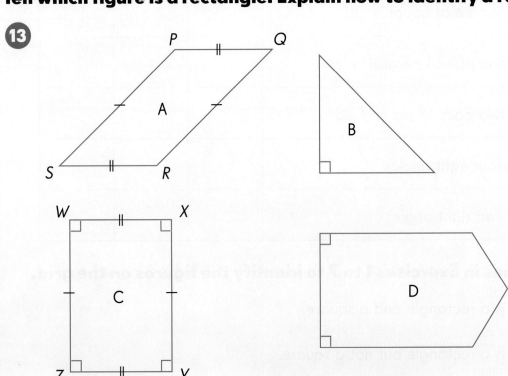

**14** **Which figure, if any, in exercise 13 is a right triangle? Explain.**

## Hands-On Activity

Use a geoboard and a rubber band
to form these figures or copy them onto
square dot paper.
Then use a drawing triangle and a protractor
to help you identify the shapes.
Which figures are squares?
Which figures are rectangles?
Which figure is a right triangle?

**Materials:**
- geoboard
- rubber band
- square dot paper
- drawing triangle
- protractor

**1**
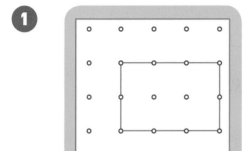

**2**
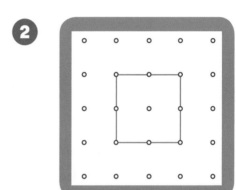

**3**
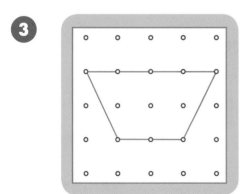

**4**
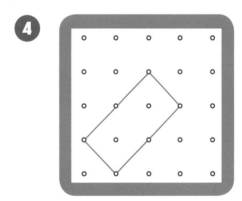

**5**
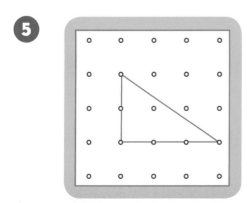

**6**
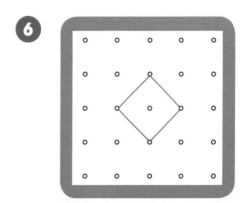

## Guided Learning

### Find the lengths of the unknown sides.

**15** Figure *JKLM* is a square.

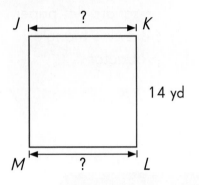

$JK = \boxed{\phantom{00}}$ yd

$LM = \boxed{\phantom{00}}$ yd

**16** Figure *PQRS* is a rectangle.

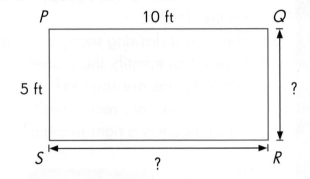

$QR = \boxed{\phantom{00}}$ ft

$RS = \boxed{\phantom{00}}$ ft

---

**Learn** **Some figures can be broken up into squares and rectangles.**

This figure can be broken up into one square and one rectangle.

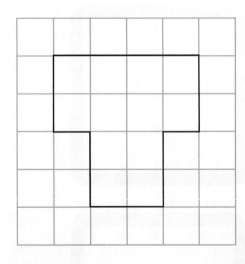

Can you break up the figure in another way?

---

# Guided Learning

**Copy these figures on grid paper.**
**Draw line segments to break up each figure into square(s) and rectangle(s).**

**17**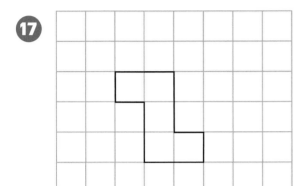

**18**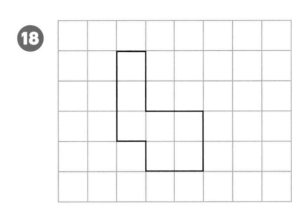

 **Hands-On Activity**

**1** Use a geoboard and two rubber bands. Form a figure that is made up of a square and a rectangle with no overlap.

> Materials:
> • geoboard
> • four rubber bands

**Example**

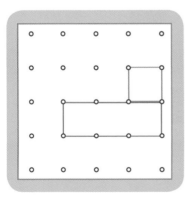

**2** Form each figure on the geoboard. Each figure should have more than four sides.

**a** a figure made up of two rectangles

**b** a figure made up of one rectangle and two squares

**c** a figure made up of one square and two rectangles

**d** a figure made up of four squares

**e** a figure made up of four rectangles

## Hands-On Activity

**WORK IN PAIRS**

Material:
- strips of centimeter grid paper

1. Use strips of paper with these lengths:
4 cm, 4 cm, 4 cm, 4 cm, 6 cm, 6 cm, 6 cm, 6 cm, 8 cm, 8 cm.

   **STEP 1** Use your strips to form two squares and two rectangles.
   Use only one or two strips to form each side of the shapes.

   **STEP 2** Draw the shapes on a piece of paper.
   Label the lengths of the sides.

   **STEP 3** Compare your shapes with the shapes formed
   by the other groups.
   How many different sizes of squares and rectangles
   can you find?

2. Use a computer drawing tool to draw these figures.
Each figure is formed by a square and a rectangle.

   **Tech Connection**

a

b

c

d

# Let's Practice

**Identify the squares, rectangles, and right triangles.**

**1**

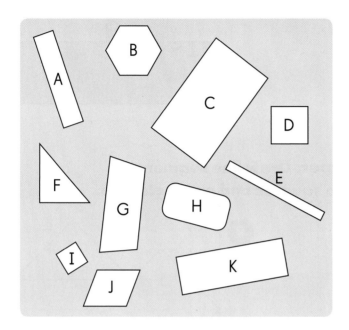

**Find the lengths of the unknown sides of the squares and rectangles.**

**2**

A  5 cm  B

D        C

AD = ⬚ cm

BC = ⬚ cm

DC = ⬚ cm

**3**

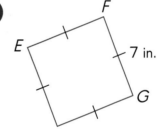

EF = ⬚ in.

EH = ⬚ in.

HG = ⬚ in.

**4**

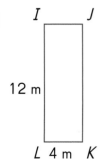

I      J

12 m

L  4 m  K

IJ = ⬚ m

JK = ⬚ m

**5**

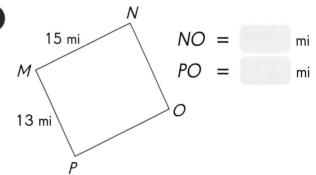

N

15 mi

M

13 mi

O

P

NO = ⬚ mi

PO = ⬚ mi

**Copy these figures on grid paper. Draw a line segment
to break up each figure into a square and a rectangle.**

**6**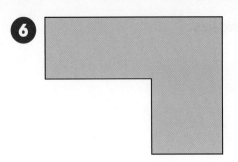

**7**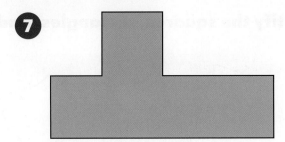

**Copy these figures on grid paper. Draw line segments
to break up each figure into two squares and one rectangle.**

**8**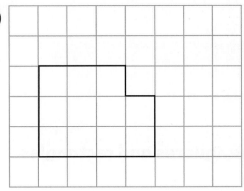

**9**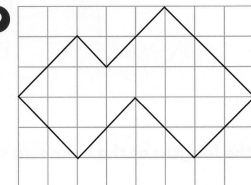

**Copy these figures on grid paper. Draw line segments
to break up each figure into one square and two rectangles.**

**10**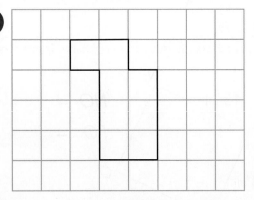

**11**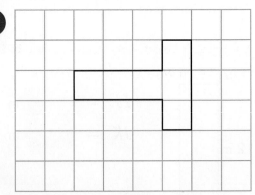

**ON YOUR OWN**

**Go to Workbook B:
Practice 1, pages 79–82**

# 11.2 Properties of Squares and Rectangles

## Lesson Objective

- Find unknown angle measures and side lengths of squares and rectangles.

**Learn** **Use the properties of squares and rectangles to find angle measures.**

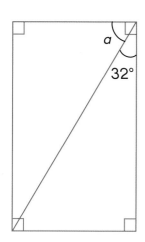

A square or a rectangle has four right angles.

Find the measure of $\angle a$.

Measure of $\angle a = 90° - 32°$
$= 58°$

## Guided Learning

**These figures may not be drawn to scale. Find the unknown measures of the angles in the square and rectangle.**

**1**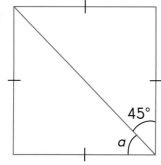

Measure of $\angle a = \boxed{\phantom{00}}°$

**2**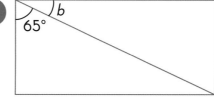

Measure of $\angle b = \boxed{\phantom{00}}°$

**These figures may not be drawn to scale. Find the unknown measures of the angles in the square and rectangle.**

 **3**

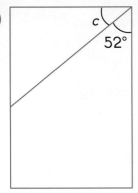

Measure of ∠c = [ ] °

 **4**

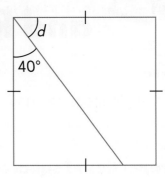

Measure of ∠d = [ ] °

**Learn** **Use the properties of squares and rectangles to find the side lengths of figures.**

Figure *ABCDEF* is made up of two rectangles. Find *BC*.

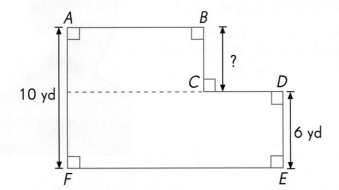

$BC = 10 - 6$
$\quad\ = 4$ yd

> The opposite sides of a rectangle are of equal length.

Figure *GHIJKL* is made up of a square and a rectangle.
Find *IJ*.

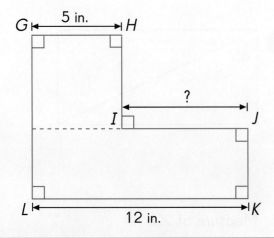

$IJ = 12 - 5$
$\quad\ = 7$ in.

> The sides of a square are of equal length.

# Guided Learning

**Find the length of the unknown side in each figure.**

**5**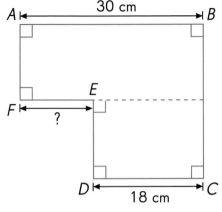

$FE = $ _____ cm

**6**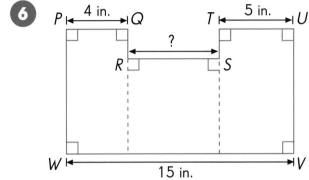

$RS = $ _____ in.

**All line segments in these figures meet at right angles.
Find the length of the unknown side in each figure.**

**7**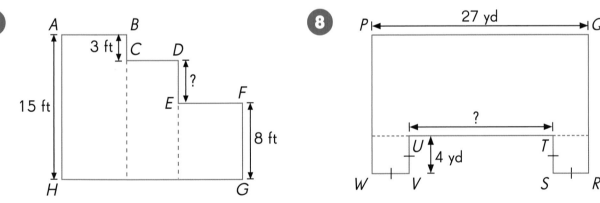

$DE = $ _____ ft

**8**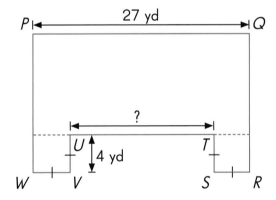

$UT = $ _____ yd

# Hands-On Activity

**Material:**
• centimeter grid paper

On grid paper, draw two different figures made up of squares and rectangles.

1 Find the perimeter of each figure.

2 Write the length of each side of the figures.

### Example

The perimeter of each figure is 16 centimeters.

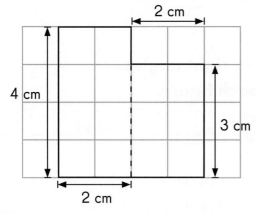

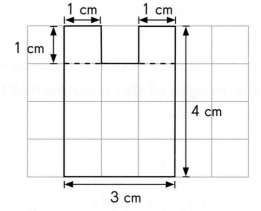

3 Draw more lines on each figure to form the smallest possible rectangle to enclose it.

4 Find the perimeter of each rectangle.

5 Compare the perimeter of each figure with the perimeter of the rectangle that encloses it.

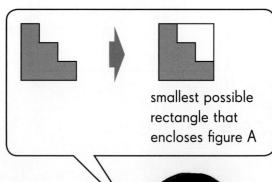

smallest possible rectangle that encloses figure A

## Let's Practice

**These figures may not be drawn to scale. Find the unknown measures of the angles in each square or rectangle.**

**1** *ABCD* is a square. Find the measure of ∠*a*.

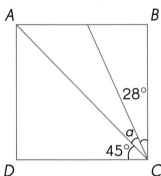

Measure of ∠*a* = ⬚ °

**2** *PQRS* is a rectangle. The measure of ∠*PQS* is 32° and the measure of ∠*SPX* is 48°. Find the measures of ∠*a*, ∠*b*, and ∠*c*.

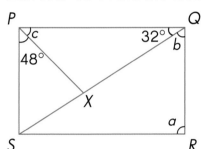

Measure of ∠*a* = ⬚ °

Measure of ∠*b* = ⬚ °

Measure of ∠*c* = ⬚ °

**All the line segments in these figures meet at right angles.**
**Find the lengths of the unknown sides in each figure.**

**3**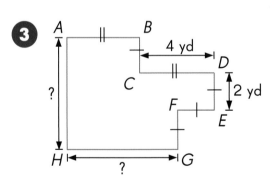

AH = ⬚ yd

HG = ⬚ yd

**4**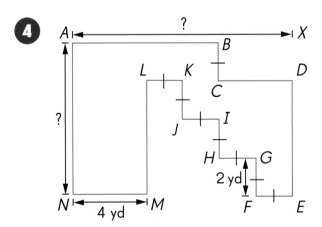

AX = ⬚ yd   AN = ⬚ yd

**ON YOUR OWN**

**Go to Workbook B:**
**Practice 2, pages 83–89**

# Put On Your Thinking Cap!

## PROBLEM SOLVING

**1** Find 8 sticks you must remove to leave behind 2 squares.

**2** Use squares and rectangles of these sizes.

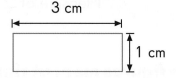

**a** How many of these squares and rectangles can you use to form a square with 3-centimeter sides?

**b** How many of these squares and rectangles can you use to form a rectangle with a length of 4 centimeters and a width of 3 centimeters?

**ON YOUR OWN**

**Go to Workbook B:
Put On Your Thinking Cap!
pages 90–92**

# Chapter Wrap Up

## Study Guide

**You have learned...**

**BIG IDEA**
▶ Squares and rectangles are four-sided figures with special properties.

### Squares and Rectangles

### Properties of Squares

- four sides of equal length
- opposite sides that are parallel
- four right angles
- a special type of rectangle

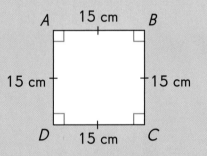

$\overline{AB} \parallel \overline{DC}$ and $\overline{AD} \parallel \overline{BC}$

### Properties of Rectangles

- four sides
- opposite sides that are of equal length and parallel
- four right angles
- may or may not be a square

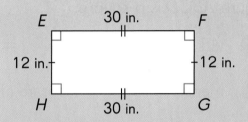

$\overline{EF} \parallel \overline{HG}$ and $\overline{FG} \parallel \overline{EH}$

Some figures are made up of squares and rectangles.

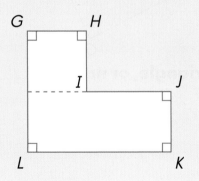

### Find Unknown Measurements

Find side lengths and angle measures in squares and rectangles.

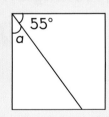

Measure of $\angle a$
$= 90° − 55°$
$= 35°$

Find lengths in figures made up of squares and rectangles.

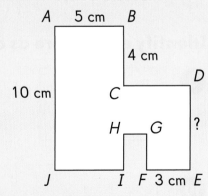

$DE = 10 − 4$
$= 6$ cm

# Chapter Review/Test

## Vocabulary

### Choose the correct word.

square

rectangle

parallel

**1** A four-sided figure with four right angles, and all sides of equal length is a _____.

**2** A four-sided figure with opposite sides of equal length, and four right angles is a _____.

## Concepts and Skills

### Complete.

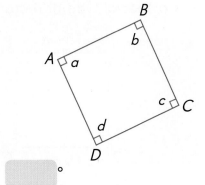

Figure *ABCD* is a square.

**3** *AB* = _____ = _____ = _____

**4** Measure of ∠*a* = measure of ∠ _____

= measure of ∠ _____ = measure of ∠ _____ = _____°

Figure *EFGH* is a rectangle.

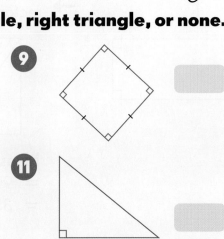

**5** *EF* = _____

**6** *EH* = _____

**7** Measure of ∠*e* = measure of ∠ _____ = _____°

## Identify each figure as a square, rectangle, right triangle, or none.

**8**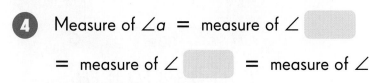

**9**

**10**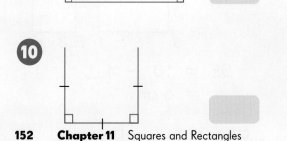

**11**

# Problem Solving

## These figures may not be drawn to scale. Solve.

**12** ABCD is a square. Find the measures of ∠b and ∠d, and AD.

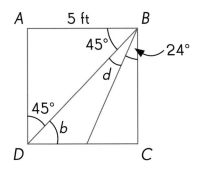

Measure of ∠b = ☐ °

Measure of ∠d = ☐ °

AD = ☐ ft

**13** WXYZ is a rectangle. Find the measures of ∠ZXY and ∠XWO, and YZ.

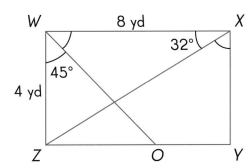

Measure of ∠ZXY = ☐ °

Measure of ∠XWO = ☐ °

YZ = ☐ yd

**14** The figure is made up of a rectangle and a square.
Find AH and FE.

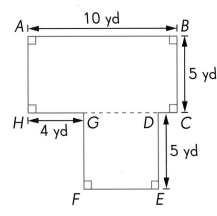

AH = ☐ yd

FE = ☐ yd

# Chapter

# 12 Conversion of Measurements

Kids, can you help me weigh the vegetables? We have to use the food scale to weigh them.

The weight of the potatoes is 5 kg.

How much is that in grams?

## Lessons

**12.1** Length
**12.2** Mass, Weight, and Volume
**12.3** Time
**12.4** Real-World Problems: Measurement

**BIG IDEA**

▶ Measurement is a way of assigning numbers to objects, such as by their length, weight, or volume. Then they can be compared.

# Recall Prior Knowledge

## Adding fractions

$\frac{1}{2} + \frac{1}{4} = \frac{2}{4} + \frac{1}{4}$

$\qquad\quad = \frac{3}{4}$

## Multiplying a fraction by a whole number

$\frac{3}{4} \times 24 = \frac{3 \times 24}{4}$

$\qquad\qquad = \frac{72}{4}$

$\qquad\qquad = 18$

## Dividing whole numbers

$725 \div 4 = 181 \text{ R } 1$

```
      1 8 1
  4) 7 2 5
     4
     ─────
     3 2
     3 2
     ─────
         5
         4
       ───
         1
```

Continued on next page

$$1{,}245 \div 60 = 20 \text{ R } 45$$

$$
\begin{array}{r}
20\phantom{0} \\
60\overline{)1\,2\,4\,5} \\
\underline{1\,3\,0\phantom{0}} \\
4\,5 \\
\underline{0} \\
4\,5
\end{array}
$$

 **Quick Check**

## Add.

**1** $\frac{1}{3} + \frac{5}{12} = \boxed{\phantom{xx}}$

**2** $\frac{5}{6} + \frac{2}{3} = \boxed{\phantom{xx}}$

**3** $\frac{5}{8} + \frac{1}{4} = \boxed{\phantom{xx}}$

## Multiply.

**4** $\frac{3}{8} \times 56 = \boxed{\phantom{xx}}$

**5** $\frac{5}{6} \times 33 = \boxed{\phantom{xx}}$

**6** $\frac{4}{5} \times 90 = \boxed{\phantom{xx}}$

## Divide the whole numbers.

**7** $789 \div 12 = \boxed{\phantom{xx}} \text{ R } \boxed{\phantom{xx}}$

**8** $1{,}445 \div 15 = \boxed{\phantom{xx}} \text{ R } \boxed{\phantom{xx}}$

# Lesson 12.1 Length

## Lesson Objectives

- Understand the relative sizes of measurement units.
- Convert metric units of length.
- Convert customary units of length, weight, and volume.

Vocabulary

| Vocabulary | |
| --- | --- |
| meter | inch |
| centimeter | mile |
| kilometer | yard |
| foot | |

### Learn Use metric length to measure.

| Metric Units of Length |
| --- |
| 1 **meter** (m) = 100 **centimeters** (cm) |
| 1 **kilometer** (km) = 1,000 meters (m) |

Which unit would you use to measure these lengths?

**a** The distance between your home and school.

Use kilometers, because this unit is used to measure long distances, like those between cities or places within a city. A kilometer is a little longer than $\frac{1}{2}$ mile.

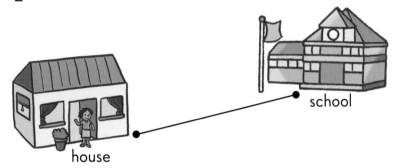

house                    school

Continued on next page

**b** The height of a tree

Use meters, because this unit is used to measure heights and lengths of buildings, trees, and other large objects. A meter is a little longer than 1 yard.

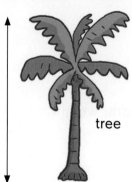

tree

**c** Your height

Use centimeters, because centimeters are short distances, a little longer than $\frac{1}{2}$ inch.

---

**Learn  Convert meters to centimeters.**

**a** 2 meters = ___?___ centimeters

1 m → 100 cm

2 m → 2 × 100

= 200 cm

So, 2 meters = 200 centimeters.

**b** $\frac{1}{2}$ meter = ___?___ centimeters

1 m → 100 cm

$\frac{1}{2}$ m → $\frac{1}{2}$ × 100 cm

= $\frac{100}{2}$ cm

= 50 cm

So, $\frac{1}{2}$ meter = 50 centimeters.

# Guided Learning

## Convert meters to centimeters.

**1** $\frac{7}{8}$ meter = ___?___ centimeters

1 m → ☐ cm

$\frac{7}{8}$ m → ☐ × ☐ cm

= ☐ cm

So, $\frac{7}{8}$ meter = ☐ centimeters.

**2** 55 meters = ___?___ centimeters

1 m → ☐ cm

55 m → ☐ × ☐ cm

= ☐ cm

So, 55 meters = ☐ centimeters.

## Convert kilometers to meters.

**a** 3 kilometers = ___?___ meters

> Rule: Multiply the number of kilometers by 1,000.

1 km → 1,000 m

3 km → 3 × 1,000

= 3,000 m

So, 3 kilometers = 3,000 meters.

**b** $\frac{1}{5}$ kilometer = ___?___ meters

1 km → 1,000 m

$\frac{1}{5}$ km → $\frac{1}{5}$ × 1,000

= $\frac{1,000}{5}$

= 200 m

So, $\frac{1}{5}$ kilometer = 200 meters.

# Guided Learning

## Convert kilometers to meters.

**3** 8 kilometers = ___?___ meters

1 km → [    ] m

8 km → [    ] × [    ] m

= [    ] m

So, 8 kilometers = [    ] meters.

**4** $\frac{3}{4}$ kilometer = ___?___ meters

1 km → [    ] m

$\frac{3}{4}$ km → [    ] × [    ] m

= [    ] m

= [    ] m

So, $\frac{3}{4}$ kilometer = [    ] meters.

---

### Learn — Use customary length to measure.

| Customary Units of Length |
|---|
| 1 **foot** (ft) = 12 inches (in.) |
| 1 **yard** (yd) = 3 feet (ft) |
| 1 **mile** (mi) = 1,760 yards (yd) |
| 1 **mile** (mi) = 5,280 feet (ft) |

You use different units of length to measure different kinds of distances. Here are some distances you might measure with each unit.

Miles → distances between cities or places with a city

Yards → distances on a football field or at a track meet

Feet → dimensions of a room or a person's height

Inches → dimensions of a book or a dinner plate

## Learn **Convert larger units to smaller units.**

**ⓐ** 12 feet = ___?___ inches

1 foot → 12 inches

12 feet → 12 × 12

       = 144 inches

So, 12 feet = 144 inches.

**ⓑ** $\frac{1}{2}$ yard = ___?___ feet

1 yard → 3 feet

$\frac{1}{2}$ yard → $\frac{1}{2}$ × 3 = $1\frac{1}{2}$ feet

So, $\frac{1}{2}$ yard = $1\frac{1}{2}$ feet.

When you convert from a larger unit to a smaller unit, you need more of the smaller units. So multiply.

## Learn **Convert miles to feet.**

2 miles = ___?___ feet

1 mile → 5,280 feet

2 miles → 2 × 5,280

      = 10,560 feet

So, 2 miles = 10,560 feet.

## Guided Learning
### Convert miles to feet.

⑤ $\frac{3}{4}$ mile = ___?___ feet

1 mile → ⬜ feet

⬜ mile → ⬜ × ⬜ feet

= ⬜ feet

= ⬜

= ⬜

So, $\frac{3}{4}$ mile = ⬜ feet.

### Learn Convert smaller units to larger units.

ⓐ 79 inches = ___?___ feet
12 inches → 1 feet
79 ÷ 12 = 6 R 7

```
      6
1 2 ) 7 9
      7 2
        7
```

So, 79 inches = 6 feet 7 inches.

How many sets of 12 inches are in 78 inches?

ⓑ 35 feet = ___?___ yards
3 feet → 1 yard
35 ÷ 3 = 11 R 2

```
      1 1
3 ) 3 5
    3
    5
    3
    2
```

**Check:**
11 groups of 3 + 2
= 3 × 11 + 2
= 33 + 2 = 35

So, 35 feet = 11 yards 2 feet.

**c** 9,245 feet = ___?___ miles

5,280 feet → 1 mile

9,245 − 5,280 = 3,965

So, 9,245 feet = 1 mile 3,965 feet.

Since, 9,245 is close 5,280, you can use the repeated subtraction method.

**Check:** 1 group of 5,280 + 3,965
= 5,280 + 3,965
= 9,245

## Guided Learning

### Convert 5,476 yards to miles.

**6** 5,476 yards = ___?___ miles

1,760 yards → 1 mile [  ] yards

[  ] − 1,760 = [  ]

[  ] − 1,760 = [  ]

[  ] − 1,760 = [  ]

So, 5,476 yards = [  ] miles [  ] yards.

How many sets of 1,760 yards are in 5,476 yards? You can use the repeated subtraction method.

**Check:** [  ] groups of 1,760 + [  ] = [  ]

# Let's Practice

## Convert meters to centimeters.

**1**

| Meters | 1 | 2 | 3 | 4 | 5 | 6 | 7 |
|---|---|---|---|---|---|---|---|
| Centimeters | | | | | | | |

## Convert kilometers to meters.

**2**

| Kilometers | 1 | 2 | 3 | 4 | 5 | 6 | 7 |
|---|---|---|---|---|---|---|---|
| Meters | | | | | | | |

## Convert feet to inches.

**3**

| Feet | 4 | 15 | $\frac{3}{4}$ | $\frac{1}{2}$ |
|---|---|---|---|---|
| Inches | | | | |

## Convert yards to feet.

**4**

| Yards | 9 | 17 | $\frac{1}{9}$ | $\frac{5}{12}$ |
|---|---|---|---|---|
| Feet | | | | |

## Convert miles to feet.

**5**

| Miles | 8 | 23 | $\frac{1}{4}$ | $\frac{3}{8}$ |
|---|---|---|---|---|
| Feet | | | | |

## Convert miles to yards.

**6**

| Miles | 7 | 15 | $\frac{3}{4}$ | $\frac{1}{2}$ |
|---|---|---|---|---|
| Yards | | | | |

**Convert inches to feet and inches.**

7.

| Inches | 84 | 147 | 258 | 512 |
|---|---|---|---|---|
| Feet and inches | | | | |

**Convert feet to yards and feet.**

8.

| Feet | 38 | 66 | 89 | 147 |
|---|---|---|---|---|
| Yards and feet | | | | |

**Convert feet to miles and feet.**

9.

| Feet | 6,125 | 10,300 | 12,478 | 9,999 |
|---|---|---|---|---|
| Miles and feet | | | | |

**Convert yards to miles and yards.**

10.

| Yards | 2,000 | 3,274 | 5,213 | 6,784 |
|---|---|---|---|---|
| Miles and yards | | | | |

ON YOUR OWN

**Go to Workbook B:
Practice 1, pages 99–108**

## Mass, Weight, and Volume

### Lesson Objectives

- Understand the relative sizes of measurement units.
- Convert metric units of mass and volume.
- Convert customary units of weight and volume.

### Vocabulary

| | |
|---|---|
| kilogram | ton |
| gram | liter |
| pound | milliliter |
| ounce | |

---

**earn** **Use metric units to measure mass.**

| **Metric Units of Mass** |
|---|
| 1 **kilogram** (kg) = 1,000 **grams** (g) |

Grams are used to measure things like the mass of fruits, vegetables, or medicines.

Kilograms are used to measure the mass of things like people and animals.

---

**earn** **Convert kilograms to grams.**

4 kilograms = ___?___ grams

Rule: Multiply the number of kilometers by 1,000.

4 kg = 4 × 1,000

     = 4,000 g

So, 4 kilograms = 4,000 grams.

# Guided Learning

## Convert kilograms to grams.

**1** $\frac{5}{8}$ kilogram = ___?___ grams

1 kg → ☐ g

$\frac{5}{8}$ kg → ☐ × ☐

= ☐ g

So, $\frac{5}{8}$ kilogram = ☐ grams.

**2** 15 kilograms = ___?___ grams

1 kg → ☐ g

15 kg → ☐ × ☐

= ☐ g

So, 15 kilograms = ☐ grams.

---

**Learn** Use customary units to measure weight.

| Customary Units of Weight |
| --- |
| 1 **pound** (lb) = 16 **ounces** (oz) |
| 1 ton = 2,000 pounds (lb) |

Tons are used to weigh things like tractors.

Pounds are used to weigh people and animals.

Ounces are used to weigh things like fruits, vegetables, and cleaning liquids.

**Convert larger units to smaller units.**

**a** 2 pounds = ___?___ ounces

1 lb → 16 oz

2 lb → 2 × 16

= 32 oz

So, 2 pounds = 32 ounces.

**b** $\frac{1}{4}$ ton = ___?___ pounds

1 ton → 2,000 lb

$\frac{1}{4}$ ton → $\frac{1}{4}$ × 2,000

= $\frac{2,000}{4}$

= 500 lb

So, $\frac{1}{4}$ ton = 500 pounds.

Check:
$\frac{500}{2,000} = \frac{100}{400}$
$= \frac{1}{4}$

## Guided Learning

**Convert larger units to smaller units.**

**3** 7 pounds = ___?___ ounces

1 lb → ⬜ oz

7 lb → ⬜ × ⬜

= ⬜ oz

So, 7 pounds = ⬜ ounces.

**4** $\frac{7}{8}$ ton = ___?___ pounds

1 ton → ⬜ lb

$\frac{7}{8}$ ton → ⬜ × ⬜

= ⬜ lb

So, $\frac{7}{8}$ ton = ⬜ pounds.

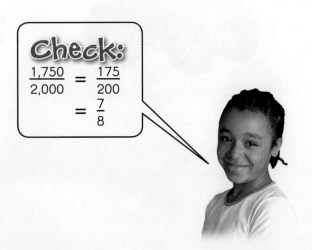

Check:
$\frac{1,750}{2,000} = \frac{175}{200}$
$= \frac{7}{8}$

**ⓐ** 45 ounces = ___?___ pounds ___?___ ounces

1 lb → 16 oz

45 ÷ 16 = 2 R 13

So, 45 ounces = 2 pounds 13 ounces

$$\begin{array}{r} 2 \phantom{0} \\ 16\overline{)4\ 5} \\ \underline{3\ 2} \\ 1\ 3 \end{array}$$

**Check:**

2 × 16 + 13 = 32 + 13
            = 45

**ⓑ** 6,750 pounds = ___?___ tons ___?___ pounds

1 ton → 2,000 pounds

6,750 ÷ 2,000 = 3 R 750

So, 6,750 pounds = 3 tons 750 pounds

$$\begin{array}{r} 3 \\ 2,000\overline{)6,7\,5\,0} \\ \underline{6\,0\,0\,0} \\ 7\,5\,0 \end{array}$$

**Check:** 3 × 2,000 + 750 = 6,750

## Guided Learning

**Convert smaller units to larger units.**

**5** 78 ounces = ___?___ pounds ___?___ ounces

1 lb → [ ] oz

78 ÷ 16 = [ ] R [ ]

So, 78 ounces = [ ] pounds [ ] ounces.

**Check:** [ ] × [ ] + [ ] = [ ]

**6** 9,425 lb = __?__ tons __?__ lb

1 ton → ▢ lb

9,425 ÷ ▢ = ▢ R ▢

So, 9,425 pounds = ▢ tons ▢ pounds.

Check: ▢ × ▢ + ▢ = ▢

---

ᴸᵉᵃʳⁿ **Use metric units to measure volume.**

| Metric Units of Volume |
|---|
| 1 **liter** (L) = 1,000 **milliliters** (mL) |

Liters are used to measure large volumes of liquids, such as amounts of fuel. Milliliters are used to measure small amount of liquids, such as beverages.

---

ᴸᵉᵃʳⁿ **Convert liters to mililiters.**

$\frac{7}{8}$ liter = __?__ milliliters

1 L → 1,000 mL

$\frac{7}{8}$ L → $\frac{7}{8}$ × 1,000 mL

= 875 mL

So, $\frac{7}{8}$ liter = 875 milliliters.

## Guided Learning

**Convert liters into milliliters.**

**7** $\frac{5}{8}$ liters = ___?___ milliliters

$1 \text{ L} \rightarrow$ [ ] mL

$\frac{5}{8} \text{ L} \rightarrow$ [ ] × [ ]

= [ ]

= [ ] mL

So, $\frac{5}{8}$ liter = [ ] milliliters

---

**ᴸᵉᵃʳⁿ Use customary unit to measure volume.**

| Customary Units of Volume |
| --- |
| 1 **gallon** (gal) = 4 quarts (qt) |
| 1 **quart** = 2 pints (pt) |
| 1 **pint** = 2 cups |
| 1 **cup** = 8 **fluid ounces** (fl oz) |

A gallon is used to measure amounts of fuel, such as gasoline.

Quarts, pints, and fluid ounces are used to measure the capacities of beverage containers.

The amount of liquid needed for a recipe is often measured in cups.

**a** 5 gallons = ___?___ quarts

1 gal → 4 qt

5 gal → 5 × 4

= 20 qt

So, 5 gallons = 20 quarts.

**b** $8\frac{1}{2}$ pints = ___?___ cups

1 pt → 2 c

$\frac{1}{2}$ pt → 1 c

8 pt → 8 × 2

= 16 c

So, $8\frac{1}{2}$ pints = 1 + 16

= 17 cups.

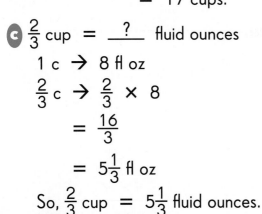

You can break up $8\frac{1}{2}$ pints into 8 pints and $\frac{1}{2}$ pints.

**c** $\frac{2}{3}$ cup = ___?___ fluid ounces

1 c → 8 fl oz

$\frac{2}{3}$ c → $\frac{2}{3}$ × 8

= $\frac{16}{3}$

= $5\frac{1}{3}$ fl oz

So, $\frac{2}{3}$ cup = $5\frac{1}{3}$ fluid ounces.

## Guided Learning

**Convert larger units to smaller units.**

**8** $7\frac{1}{2}$ gallons = ___?___ quarts

1 gal → ▢ qt

$\frac{1}{2}$ gal → ▢ qt

7 gal → ▢ qt

$7\frac{1}{2}$ gal → ▢ qt + ▢ qt

So, $7\frac{1}{2}$ gallons = ▢ quarts.

**9** 18 quarts = ___?___ pints

1 qt → 2 pt

18 qt → [ ] × [ ]

     = [ ] pt

So, 18 quarts = [ ] pints.

**10** $3\frac{1}{4}$ cups = ___?___ fluid ounces

1 c → 8 fl oz

$\frac{1}{4}$ c → [ ] × [ ]

     = [ ] fl oz

3 c → [ ] fl oz

$3\frac{1}{4}$ c = [ ] + [ ] fl oz

So, $3\frac{1}{4}$ cups = [ ] fluid ounces.

## Convert smaller units to larger units.

**a** 9 quarts = ___?___ gallons ___?___ quarts

1 gal → 4 qt

9 ÷ 4 = 2 remainder 1

So, 9 quarts = 2 gallons 1 quart.

$$\begin{array}{r} 2 \\ 4\overline{)9} \\ \underline{8} \\ 1 \end{array}$$

**Check:** 2 × 4 + 1 = 8 + 1 = 9

**b** 23 pints = ___?___ quarts ___?___ pints

1 qt → 2 pt

23 ÷ 2 = 11 R 1

So, 23 pints = 11 quarts 1 pint.

$$\begin{array}{r} 1\ 1 \\ 2\overline{)2\ 3} \\ \underline{2} \\ 3 \\ \underline{2} \\ 1 \end{array}$$

**Check:** 2 × 11 + 1 = 22 + 1 = 23

Continued on next page

**c** 78 pints = __?__ gallons __?__ quarts

1 qt → 2 pt

78 ÷ 2 = 39

So, 78 pints = 39 quarts.

$$\begin{array}{r} 3\ 9 \\ 2\overline{)7\ 8} \\ \underline{6} \\ 1\ 8 \\ \underline{1\ 8} \\ 0 \end{array}$$

1 gal → 4 qt

39 ÷ 4 = 9 R 3

So, 78 pints = 9 gallons 3 quarts.

$$\begin{array}{r} 9 \\ 4\overline{)3\ 9} \\ \underline{3\ 6} \\ 3 \end{array}$$

**Check:** 9 × 8 + 3 × 2 = 72 + 6
= 78

## Guided Learning

### Convert smaller units to larger units.

**11** 35 pints = __?__ quarts __?__ pints

1 qt → [    ] pt

35 ÷ [    ] = [    ] R [    ]

So, 35 pints = [    ] quarts [    ] pints.

**Check:** [    ] × [    ] + [    ] = [    ] + [    ] = [    ]

**12** 105 pints = __?__ gallons __?__ quarts __?__ pints

1 qt → [    ] pt

105 ÷ [    ] = [    ] R [    ]

So, 105 pints = [    ] quarts [    ] pints.

1 gal → 4 qt

[    ] ÷ 4 = [    ] R [    ]

So, 105 pints = [    ] gallon [    ] quarts [    ] pints.

# Let's Practice

## Convert kilograms to grams.

**1**

| Kilograms | 1 | 2 | 3 | 4 | 5 | 6 |
|-----------|---|---|---|---|---|---|
| Grams | | | | | | |

## Convert pounds to ounces.

**2**

| Pounds | 9 | 16 | $\frac{1}{4}$ | $\frac{3}{8}$ |
|--------|---|----|---------------|---------------|
| Ounces | | | | |

## Convert tons to pounds.

**3**

| Tons | 7 | 12 | $5\frac{1}{2}$ | $16\frac{3}{4}$ |
|------|---|----|----------------|-----------------|
| Pounds | | | | |

## Convert ounces to pounds and ounces.

**4**

| Ounces | 22 | 59 | 77 | 146 |
|--------|----|----|----|-----|
| Pounds and ounces | | | | |

## Convert liters to milliliters.

**5**

| Liters | 1 | 3 | 5 | 6 |
|---|---|---|---|---|
| Milliliters | | | | |

## Convert pounds to tons and pounds.

**6**

| Pounds | 2,160 | 7,285 | 8,869 | 10,435 |
|---|---|---|---|---|
| Tons and pounds | | | | |

## Convert gallons to quarts.

**7**

| Gallons | 6 | $\frac{3}{4}$ | 14 | $9\frac{1}{2}$ |
|---|---|---|---|---|
| Quarts | | | | |

## Convert quarts to pints.

**8**

| Quarts | 7 | $9\frac{1}{2}$ | 16 | 22 |
|---|---|---|---|---|
| Pints | | | | |

## Convert pints to cups.

**9**

| Pints | 5 | $7\frac{3}{4}$ | 24 | $\frac{1}{8}$ |
|---|---|---|---|---|
| Cups | | | | |

**Convert cups to fluid ounces.**

10

| Cups | 13 | $\frac{3}{8}$ | 28 | $15\frac{1}{4}$ |
|---|---|---|---|---|
| Fluid ounces | | | | |

**Convert quarts to gallons and quarts.**

11

| Quarts | 11 | 15 | 34 | 55 |
|---|---|---|---|---|
| Gallons and quarts | | | | |

**Convert pints to quarts and pints.**

12

| Pints | 8 | 13 | 27 | 45 |
|---|---|---|---|---|
| Quarts and pints | | | | |

**Convert cups to pints and cups.**

13

| Cups | 7 | 14 | 25 | 47 |
|---|---|---|---|---|
| Pints and cups | | | | |

**Convert pints to gallons, quarts, pints.**

14

| Pints | 19 | 28 | 45 | 69 |
|---|---|---|---|---|
| Gallons, quarts, and pints | | | | |

**Solve.**

**15** For one winter meeting, the hosts brewed 9 pints of cocoa and $2\frac{1}{2}$ quarts of hot apple cider. Was there more cocoa or more cider for the meeting?

**16** Mrs. Lee bought $\frac{3}{4}$ gallon of milk for $3. Mrs. Gomez bought 20 pints of milk for $6. Who gets more milk with the same amount of money?

**17** Daniel bought $1\frac{1}{2}$ gallons of gasoline for his lawn mower at a service station. Lena bought 7 quarts of gasoline at a mower shop. Who bought more gasoline? How much more? Express your answer in quarts.

**18** Tank A contains 8 gallons of kerosene. Tank B contains 88 pints of kerosene. Which tank contains more kerosene? How many quarts more?

**ON YOUR OWN**

**Go to Workbook B:**
**Practice 2, pages 109–122**

# 12.3 Time

## Lesson Objectives

- Understand the relative sizes of units of time.
- Convert units of time.

### Learn Measuring time.

| Units of Time |
|---|
| 1 **minute** (min) = 60 **seconds** (s) |
| 1 **hour** (h) = 60 minutes (min) |

Which unit would you use to measure the amount of time needed for these activities? Might you use more than one unit to talk about the time any of these activities take?

- Eating lunch
- A trip to the zoo
- Sneezing

### Learn Convert larger units to smaller units.

**a** 2 minutes = ___?___ seconds

1 min → 60 s

2 min → 2 × 60

= 120 s

So 2 minutes = 120 seconds.

Continued on next page

**b** $5\frac{3}{4}$ hours = _____?_____ minutes

1 h → 60 min

$\frac{3}{4}$ h → $\frac{3}{4}$ × 60 min

    = 45 min

5 h → 5 × 60 min

    = 300 min

$5\frac{3}{4}$ h = 300 + 45

    = 345 min

So, $5\frac{3}{4}$ hour = 345 minutes.

## Guided Learning

### Convert larger units to smaller units.

**1** 4 minutes = _____?_____ seconds

1 min → ▢ s

4 min → ▢ × ▢

    = ▢ s

So, 4 minutes = ▢ seconds.

**2** $\frac{2}{5}$ hour = _____?_____ minutes

1 h → ▢ min

$\frac{2}{5}$ h = ▢ × ▢ min

    = ▢ min

So, $\frac{2}{5}$ hour = ▢ minutes.

**Learn** **Convert smaller units to larger units.**

**ⓐ** 125 seconds = ___?___ minutes ___?___ seconds

125 ÷ 60 = 2 R 5

So, 125 seconds = 2 minutes 5 seconds.

$$\begin{array}{r} 2 \\ 60\overline{)1\ 2\ 5} \\ \underline{1\ 2\ 0} \\ 5 \end{array}$$

**ⓑ** 5,285 seconds = ___?___ hours ___?___ minutes ___?___ seconds

5,285 ÷ 60 = 88 R 5

5,285 s = 88 min 5 s

88 ÷ 60 = 1 R 28

88 min = 1 h 28 min

$$\begin{array}{r} 1 \\ 60\overline{)8\ 8} \\ \underline{6\ 0} \\ 2\ 8 \end{array}$$

$$\begin{array}{r} 8\ 8 \\ 60\overline{)5,2\ 8\ 5} \\ \underline{4\ 8\ 0} \\ 4\ 8\ 5 \\ \underline{4\ 8\ 0} \\ 5 \end{array}$$

So, 5,285 seconds = 1 hour 28 minutes 5 seconds.

## Guided Learning

**Convert smaller units to larger units.**

**③** 215 seconds = ___?___ minutes ___?___ seconds

[ ] ÷ [ ] = [ ] R [ ]

So, 215 seconds = [ ] minutes [ ] seconds.

**④** 4,790 seconds = ___?___ hours ___?___ minutes ___?___ seconds

[ ] ÷ 60 = [ ] R [ ]

4,790 s = [ ] min [ ] s

[ ] ÷ 60 = [ ] R [ ]

[ ] min = [ ] h [ ] min

So, 4,790 seconds = [ ] hour [ ] minutes [ ] seconds.

## Let's Practice

**Convert the times to the given units.**

**1** 4 min = [ ] s

**2** $\frac{3}{10}$ min = [ ] s

**3** 12 h = [ ] min

**4** $8\frac{3}{4}$ h = [ ] min

**5** 2 h 3 min = [ ] min

**6** 3 h 15 min 45 s = [ ] s

**7** 215 s = [ ] min [ ] s

**8** 445 s = [ ] min [ ] s

**9** 560 min = [ ] h [ ] min

**10** 775 min = [ ] h [ ] min

**11** 3,764 s = [ ] h [ ] min [ ] s

**12** 6,680 s = [ ] h [ ] min [ ] s

**Solve.**

**13** A 14-pound turkey needs to be baked for 17 minutes per pound. How many hours and minutes does the turkey need to bake?

**14** In a relay race, a team of 4 members ran their segments for the following times: 92 seconds, 98 seconds, 102 second, and 90 seconds. How many minutes and seconds did it take the team to finish the race?

**ON YOUR OWN**

**Go to Workbook B:**
**Practice 3, pages 123–126**

# Real-World Problems: Measurement

## Lesson Objectives

- Use the four operations to solve word problems involving distance, time, volume, mass, and money.
- Represent measurement quantities using line diagrams.

### Learn Solve word problems involving distance.

Phil lives $\frac{1}{4}$ mile from school. Marissa lives further away from school. She lives $\frac{1}{2}$ mile from Phil and in the same direction from school.

**a** How many miles does Marissa live from school?

**b** How many yards does Marissa live from school?

You can use a line diagram to represent and solve the problem.

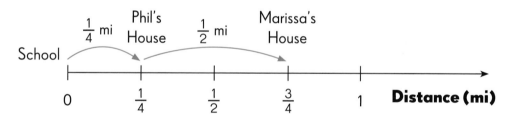

**a** Add the two distances.
$\frac{1}{4} + \frac{1}{2} = \frac{3}{4}$
Marissa lives $\frac{3}{4}$ mile from school.

**b** 1 mile = 1,760 yards

Multiply to find $\frac{3}{4}$ of 1,760 yards.

$$\frac{3}{4} \times 1,760 = \frac{3 \times 1,760}{4}$$
$$= \frac{5,280}{4}$$
$$= 1,320 \text{ yards}$$

Marissa lives 1,320 yards from school.

## Guided Learning

**1** Kenny lives $\frac{3}{8}$ of the distance from school to his friend's house. His friend lives 2 miles from school.

**a** How many miles does Kenny live from school?

[  ] × [  ] = [  ]

Kenny lives [  ] mile from school.

**b** How many yards does Kenny live from school?

1 mile → [  ] yards

[  ] mile → [  ] × [  ] = [  ] yards

Kenny lives [  ] yards from school.

---

**ᴸᵉᵃʳⁿ  Solve word problems involving time.**

Samantha's softball game on Saturday started at 9:15 A.M. and lasted 2 hours 50 minutes. At what time did the game end?

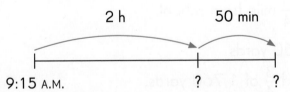

**Step 1:** Count 2 hours after 9:15 A.M.
2 hours after 9:15 A.M. is 11:15 A.M.

**Step 2:** Count 50 minutes after 11:15 A.M.
50 minutes after 11:15 A.M. is 12:05 P.M.

So, the game ended at 12:05 P.M.

---

# Guided Learning

**2** In the morning, Ellis School has four 50-minute class periods, three 5-minute passing times. Then it is time for lunch. If the school day begins at 8:30 A.M., what time does lunch start?

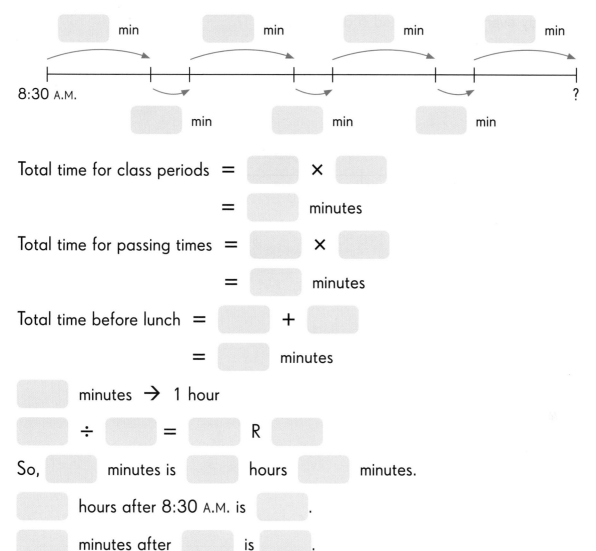

Total time for class periods = [ ] × [ ]

= [ ] minutes

Total time for passing times = [ ] × [ ]

= [ ] minutes

Total time before lunch = [ ] + [ ]

= [ ] minutes

[ ] minutes → 1 hour

[ ] ÷ [ ] = [ ] R [ ]

So, [ ] minutes is [ ] hours [ ] minutes.

[ ] hours after 8:30 A.M. is [ ] .

[ ] minutes after [ ] is [ ] .

So, lunch starts at [ ] .

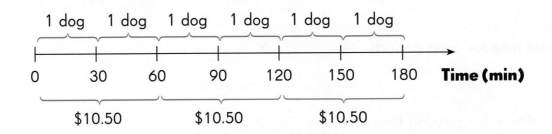

## Solve word problems involving time and money.

Louisa walks dogs after school to earn extra pocket money.
She gives each dog a 30-minute walk, walking only one dog at a time.
She earns $10.50 an hour.
On Friday evening, she walked 6 dogs.

**a** How long did Louisa take to walk all the dogs?

**b** How much did Louisa earn by walking 6 dogs?

**a** 1 dog → 30 min
6 dogs → 6 × 30 min
       = 180 min
       = 3 h

Louisa took 3 hours to walk all the dogs.

**b** 1 hour → $10.50
3 hours → 3 × $10.50
        = $31.50

Louisa earned $31.50 by walking 6 dogs.

# Guided Learning

**3** Malcolm makes wooden puzzles to sell at craft fairs. Each puzzle takes 20 minutes to cut, 40 minutes to paint, and 30 minutes to seal and finish. He thinks he should earn $12 for each hour of work. How much should he charge for his labor?

Total time taken = [    ] + [    ] + [    ]

= [    ] minutes

[    ] minutes → 1 hour

[    ] minutes → [    ] ÷ [    ] = [    ] hours

Amount he should charge for his labor = [    ] × $12

= $ [    ]

He should charge $ [    ].

---

## $^{earn}$ Solve word problems involving volume.

Peter has four watering cans. Two blue watering cans contain $1\frac{1}{2}$ quarts water each. One red watering can contains 1 quart water, and one green watering can contains $\frac{1}{2}$ quart water.

**a** How much water does Peter have altogether?

**b** Peter uses the red watering can to water his herb garden. How many quarts of water does he have left?

**a** $1\frac{1}{2} + 1\frac{1}{2} + 1 + \frac{1}{2} = 4\frac{1}{2}$

Peter has $4\frac{1}{2}$ quarts of water altogether.

**b** $4\frac{1}{2} - 1 = 3\frac{1}{2}$

Peter has $3\frac{1}{2}$ quarts of water left.

# Guided Learning

**4** Janelle is planning to make fruit punch for a party. She thinks that she should make 12 fluid ounces of punch for each of the 14 guests.

**a** How many fluid ounces of punch does she need to make?

$$\boxed{\phantom{xx}} \times \boxed{\phantom{xx}} = \boxed{\phantom{xx}}$$

She needs to make $\boxed{\phantom{xx}}$ fluid ounces of punch.

**b** Does she need a 4-quart, 5-quart, 6-quart, or 7-quart punch bowl to hold all the punch? Explain.

$\boxed{\phantom{xx}}$ fl. oz → 1 qt

$\boxed{\phantom{xx}}$ fl. oz → $\boxed{\phantom{xx}}$ ÷ $\boxed{\phantom{xx}}$

$= \boxed{\phantom{xx}}$ R $\boxed{\phantom{xx}} = \boxed{\phantom{xx}}$ qt $\boxed{\phantom{xx}}$ fl. oz

She needs a $\boxed{\phantom{xx}}$ punch bowl.

---

**Learn** **Solve word problems involving weight.**

Ingrid buys 5 bags of apples weighing $\frac{3}{4}$ pound each.

**a** What is the total weight of all the apples in ounces?

**b** Ingrid then packs the apples equally in 10 boxes. What is the weight of each box?

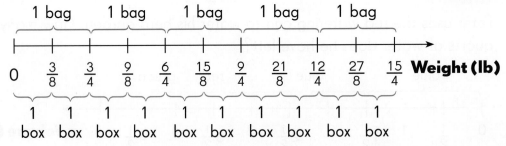

(a) $5 \times \dfrac{3}{4} = \dfrac{15}{4}$

$\qquad\qquad = 3\dfrac{3}{4}$

3 pounds $= 3 \times 16$

$\qquad\qquad = 48$ ounces

$\dfrac{3}{4}$ pound $= \dfrac{3}{4} \times 16$

$\qquad\qquad = 12$ ounces

$48 + 12 = 60$

The total weight of the apples is 60 ounces.

(b) $60 \div 10 = 6$

Each box weighs 6 ounces.

## Guided Learning

5) For a school fair, the students are buying 4 canisters of trail mix and repackaging it in small bags to sell at the snack bar. The canisters of trail mix each contain $1\dfrac{1}{2}$ pounds, and the bags they are making will contain 3 ounces. How many bags can they make?

Total amount of trail mix = ⬜ × ⬜

$\qquad\qquad\qquad\qquad$ = ⬜ pounds

1 pound = ⬜ ounces

⬜ pounds = ⬜ × ⬜

$\qquad\qquad$ = ⬜ ounces

Number of bags they can make = ⬜ ÷ ⬜

$\qquad\qquad\qquad\qquad\qquad\qquad$ = ⬜

They can make ⬜ bags.

## Let's Practice

**Copy and complete the number diagram and solve.**

**1** An helicopter makes a $1\frac{1}{2}$-hour scenic tour over the Mount Rushmore 3 days of the week. The gasoline cost for each hour is $208.

  **a** How many minutes does the helicopter spend in the air each week?

  **b** What is the gasoline cost for the three days?

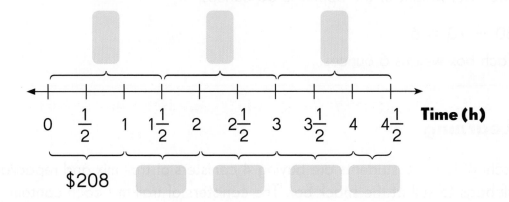

**2** Keira, Melissa, Sheila, and Emily run in a 1-mile charity relay race. Keira runs $\frac{1}{4}$ mile, Melissa runs $\frac{3}{8}$ mile, and Emily runs $\frac{1}{8}$ mile.

  **a** What fraction of the race remains for Sheila to run?

  **b** How many yards does Sheila have to run?

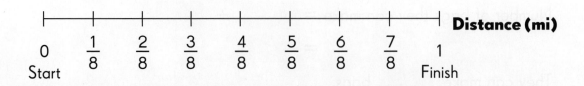

**3** Filipe fills a bottle completely with water for his rabbits. His rabbits drink $1\frac{1}{2}$ cups a day. After 4 days, the bottle is empty.

**a** How much water was in the bottle at first?

**b** Filipe fills the bottle completely again, but spills some water, leaving $5\frac{1}{4}$ cups left in the bottle. How many ounces of water did he spill?

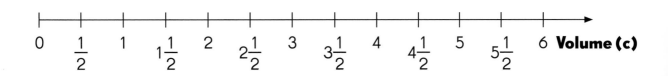

0    $\frac{1}{2}$    1    $1\frac{1}{2}$    2    $2\frac{1}{2}$    3    $3\frac{1}{2}$    4    $4\frac{1}{2}$    5    $5\frac{1}{2}$    6    **Volume (c)**

## Solve. Draw a number diagram to help you.

**4** The mass of Jayden's hamster is 100 grams. The mass of his rabbit is five times the mass of his hamster.

**a** What is the mass of Jayden's rabbit?

**b** What is the total mass of Jayden's hamster and rabbit?

**5** Mrs. Peres left the house at 9:00 A.M. and walked for 25 minutes to the grocery store. She left the grocery store 45 minutes later after shopping, and walked home again.

**a** What time did she get home?

**b** Mrs. Peres takes 10 minutes to walk a block. How many blocks did she walk altogether, to and from the grocery store?

**ON YOUR OWN**

**Go to Workbook B:**
**Practice 4, pages 127–130**

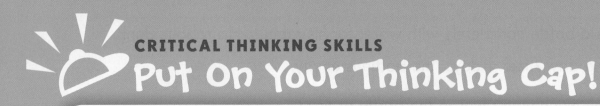

**PROBLEM SOLVING**

Ramona spends 1 hour 20 minutes doing her homework. Then, she spends 20 minutes doing chores and feeding her goldfish. Finally, she practices the saxophone for 35 minutes until 9:00 P.M.
What time did she begin doing her homework?

You can use a time line to represent and solve the problem.

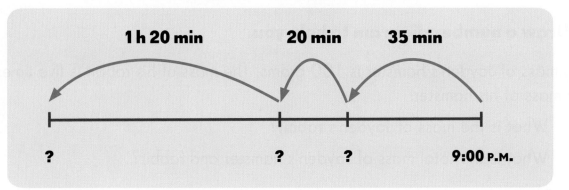

**ON YOUR OWN**

**Go to Workbook B:
Put On Your Thinking Cap!
pages 131–132**

# Chapter Wrap Up

**BIG IDEAS**

▶ Measurement is a way of assigning numbers to objects, such as by their length, weight, or volume. Then, they can be compared.

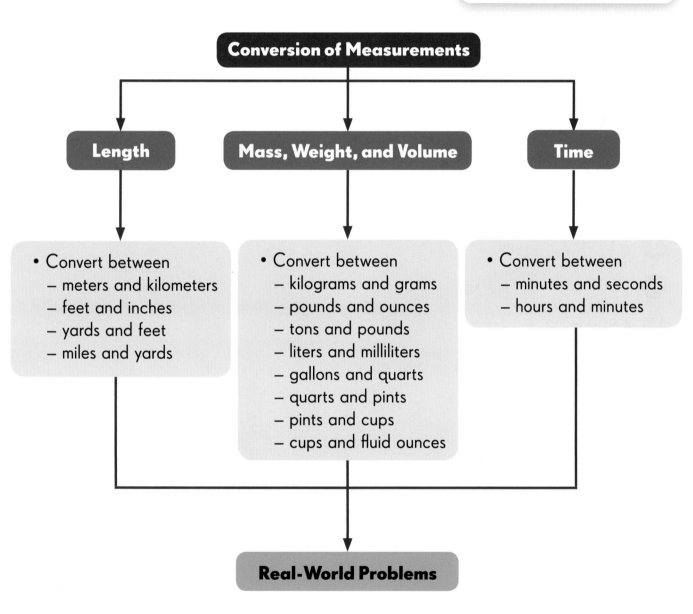

**Conversion of Measurements**

**Length**

- Convert between
  - meters and kilometers
  - feet and inches
  - yards and feet
  - miles and yards

**Mass, Weight, and Volume**

- Convert between
  - kilograms and grams
  - pounds and ounces
  - tons and pounds
  - liters and milliliters
  - gallons and quarts
  - quarts and pints
  - pints and cups
  - cups and fluid ounces

**Time**

- Convert between
  - minutes and seconds
  - hours and minutes

**Real-World Problems**

# Chapter Review/Test

## Vocabulary

**1** The height of the chair can be measured in ☐ .

**2** You can use ☐ to measure volume.

**3** An egg has a weight of about 5 ☐ .

**4** The fastest time for the 5-mile marathon was 55 ☐ .

**5** The slab of butter weighs 250 ☐ .

> ounces
>
> meters
>
> pints
>
> grams
>
> minutes

## Concepts and Skills

### Convert.

**1** 2 kg = ☐ g

**2** 3 m = ☐ cm

**3** $\frac{1}{5}$ L = ☐ mL

**4** 1,300 g = ☐ kg ☐ g

**5** 4,809 m = ☐ km ☐ m

**6** 12,750 mL = ☐ L ☐ mL

**7** $2\frac{1}{2}$ mi = ☐ ft

**8** $\frac{3}{5}$ ft = ☐ in.

**9** $4\frac{3}{4}$ mi = ☐ yd

**10** $1\frac{3}{8}$ lb = ☐ oz

**11** $1\frac{1}{5}$ ton = ☐ lb

**12** 2,350 lb = ☐ ton ☐ lb

**13** $8\frac{1}{3}$ pt = ☐ c

**14** 35 pt = ⬚ qt ⬚ pt

**15** 61 pt = ⬚ gal ⬚ qt ⬚ pt

**16** $1\frac{7}{10}$ min = ⬚ sec

**17** 712 min = ⬚ h ⬚ min

**18** 3,600 sec = ⬚ h ⬚ min ⬚ sec

## Problem Solving

**19** Casey has 37 quarts of water and Maisy has 9 gallons of water. Who has more?

**20** A man drove from Town A to Town B. He was in Town B for 45 minutes. Then he returned using the same route from Town B to Town A, at the same speed. Each way took 320 minutes. If he left Town A at 8 A.M., at what time did he return to Town A?

**21** To bake a cake, Jeremy used a pound of butter, 8 ounces of flour, 12 ounces of sugar, and 3 eggs that weighed 7 ounces each. What was the weight of the batter when all the ingredients were added? Give your answer in pounds and ounces.

**22** A box containing 5 apples weighs 1 kilogram 200 grams. The box weighs 360 grams. What is the weight of each apple if they all weigh the same?

**23** A bookcase has 5 shelves that are 10 inches apart. How tall is the bookcase in feet and inches?

**24** A porch railing has 16 vertical slats with a post at each end. The centers of the slats are 15 centimeters apart. How long is the distance between the posts in meters and centimeters?

# Area and Perimeter

Let's carpet the floor and put in a wallpaper border for the music room.

We have to find the total area of the floor. The floor can be divided into two squares.

How much carpet do we need?

Let's measure the sides of the room to find the perimeter.

What length of wallpaper border do we need?

## Lessons

### BIG IDEA

▶ Area and perimeter of a square, rectangle, or composite figure can be found by counting squares or using a formula.

### Using an area model to show multiplication facts

There are 5 groups of 7 tomatoes.
How many tomatoes are there altogether?

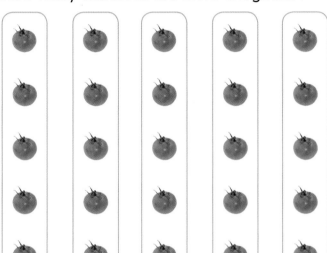

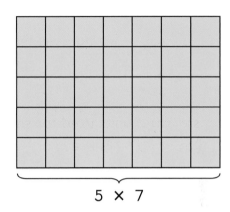

$5 \times 7$

5 groups of 7
$= 5 \times 7$
$= 7 + 7 + 7 + 7 + 7$
$= 35$

There are 35 tomatoes altogether.

### Area

The area of a figure is the amount of surface covered by the figure.

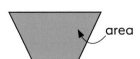
area

The standard units used for small areas are square centimeter ($cm^2$) and square inch ($in.^2$). The standard units used for large areas are square meter ($m^2$) and square foot ($ft^2$).

## Finding the area of a figure

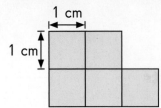

1 cm

1 cm

You can count square units to find the area.
The figure is made up of 5 one-centimeter squares.
The area of the figure is 5 cm².

## Perimeter

The perimeter of a figure is the distance around it.

perimeter

The standard units used for short distances are centimeter (cm) and inch (in.).
The standard units used for long distances are meter (m) and foot (ft).

## Finding the perimeter of a figure

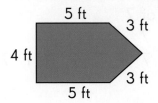

5 ft

3 ft

4 ft

3 ft

5 ft

You can add the lengths of sides to find the perimeter.
Perimeter = 5 + 3 + 3 + 5 + 4
= 20 ft
The perimeter of the figure is 20 feet.

# ✔ Quick Check

## Multiply.

**1** There are 3 boxes of 5 pencils in each box.
How many pencils are there in all?

5 pencils in a box

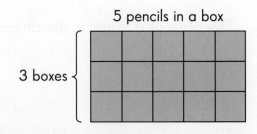

3 boxes

3 × 5 = ☐ rows of ☐

= ☐ + ☐ + ☐

= ☐

There are ☐ pencils in all.

## Trace these figures. Outline the perimeter and shade the area of each figure.

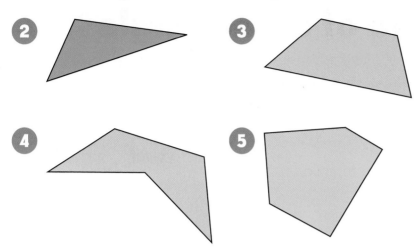

**2**

**3**

**4**

**5**

## Find the area of the figure.
## Each grid square is 1 square centimeter.

**6**

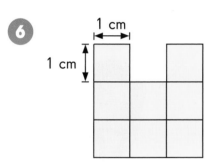

1 cm

1 cm

Area = _____ cm²

## Find the perimeter of the figure.

**7**

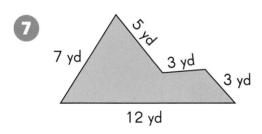

5 yd

7 yd

3 yd

3 yd

12 yd

Perimeter = _____ yd

# 13.1 Area of a Rectangle

## Lesson Objectives

- Estimate the area of a rectangle by counting grid squares.
- Find the area of a rectangle using a formula.

**Learn** **Find the area of a rectangle by counting squares.**

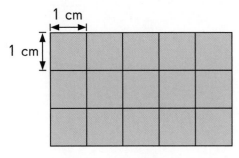

There are 3 rows of squares.
Each row has 5 squares.
There are 15 one-centimeter squares
covering the rectangle.
So, the area of the rectangle is 15 cm$^2$.

What is the area of the rectangle?
Count the one-centimeter squares
covering the rectangle to find out.

**Learn** **Find the area of a rectangle using a formula.**

The longer side of the rectangle is usually called the **length**.
The shorter side is called the **width**.

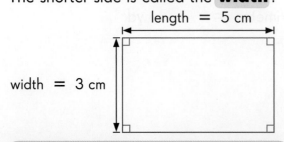

$3 \times 5 = 15$

Area of rectangle = length × width

Area = 5 × 3
     = 15 cm$^2$

Square centimeters
is abbreviated cm$^2$.

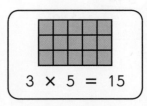

# Guided Learning

## Find the area of each rectangle.

 **1**

1 in.

1 in.

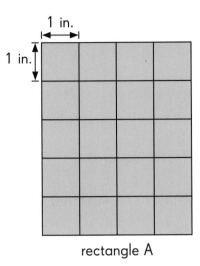

rectangle A

Count the number of one-inch squares covering rectangle A.

There are ⬚ rows of one-inch squares.

Each row has ⬚ one-inch squares.

There are ⬚ one-inch squares covering rectangle A.

Area of rectangle A = ⬚ in.²

**2**

length = 8 ft

width = 2 ft

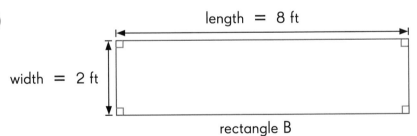

rectangle B

What is the other way to find the area of a rectangle?

Area of rectangle B = length × width

= ⬚ × ⬚

= ⬚ ft²

# Find the area of the square.

**3** Square C is covered with one-meter squares.
Find the area of square C using two different methods.

### *Method 1*

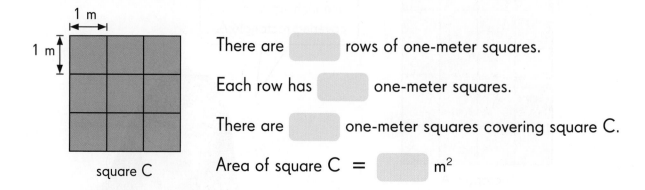

There are [ ] rows of one-meter squares.

Each row has [ ] one-meter squares.

There are [ ] one-meter squares covering square C.

Area of square C = [ ] m²

### *Method 2*

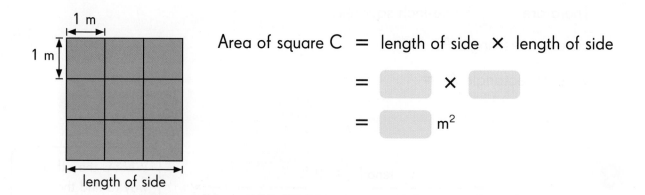

Area of square C = length of side × length of side

= [ ] × [ ]

= [ ] m²

The lengths of all sides of a square are equal.

# Find the area of each figure.

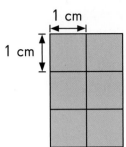

1 cm

1 cm

Area = length × width

= ⬜ × ⬜

= ⬜ cm²

⑤

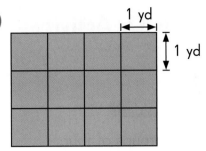

1 yd

1 yd

Area = length × width

= ⬜ × ⬜

= ⬜ yd²

# Find the area of each rectangle or square.

⑥

7 in.

3 in.

Area = ⬜ in.²

⑦

4 mi

4 mi

Area = ⬜ mi²

⑧

9 ft

2 ft

Area = ⬜ ft²

⑨

6 yd

6 yd

Area = ⬜ yd²

## Hands-On Activity

**WORKING TOGETHER**

Materials:
- geoboard
- rubber bands
- dot paper

**1** Work in groups of four.
Use a geoboard and rubber bands to make four rectangles.
Each rectangle should be a different size.
Each side should be parallel to the border of the geoboard.
Use dot paper to record your figures.

The squares formed by the pegs of a geoboard are square units.
For each rectangle,

**a** find the number of horizontal rows of square units.

**b** find the number of square units in each row.

**c** find the area using the formula.

Area = length × width

**2** Use these line segments to make three rectangles of different sizes.
Use each line segment twice. Use dot paper to record your figures.
Find the perimeter and area of each rectangle.

3 cm

4 cm

6 cm

2 cm

5 cm

7 cm

## Guided Learning

### Solve.

**10** Janel bent a 36-inch wire to make a square photo frame.
What is the area inside the photo frame?

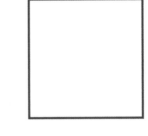

Length of one side = [          ] ÷ 4

= [          ] in.

Area inside photo frame = [          ] × [          ]

= [          ] in.²

**11** The length of one side of a square garden is 8 yards.
Half of the garden was used for growing vegetables.
What area of the garden was used for growing vegetables?

### Method 1

Half of length of one side of square garden

= [          ] ÷ 2

= [          ] yd

Area of garden used for growing vegetables

= [          ] × [          ]

= [          ] yd²

### Method 2

Area of garden = [          ] × 8

= [          ] yd²

Area of garden used for growing vegetables = [          ] ÷ 2

= [          ] yd²

Use rounding to estimate the areas of the figures.

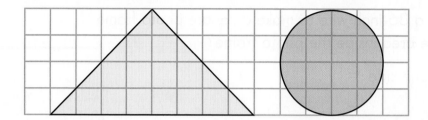

| Shaded Region | Area of Shaded Region | Approximate Area |
|:---:|:---:|:---:|
| ▢ | 1 square unit | 1 square unit |
| ◺ | $\frac{1}{2}$ square unit | $\frac{1}{2}$ square unit |
| | greater than $\frac{1}{2}$ square unit | 1 square unit |
| | less than $\frac{1}{2}$ square unit | 0 square unit |

Look at the triangle. Count the squares.

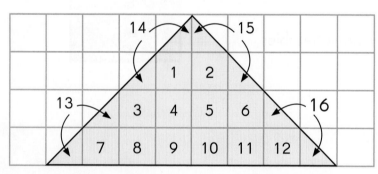

The area of the triangle is 16 square units.

Look at the circle. Count the squares.

The area of the circle is about 12 square units.

# Guided Learning

## Estimate the area of each figure. Count the square units.

| | | | | | | |
|---|---|---|---|---|---|---|
| ⬛ | Count 1 square unit. | ◩ | Count $\frac{1}{2}$ square unit. | ◰ | Count 1 square unit. | ◱ | Count 0 square units. |

**12**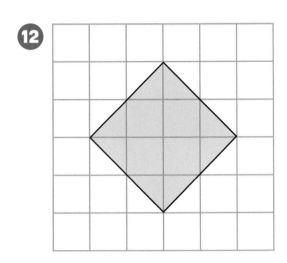

**13**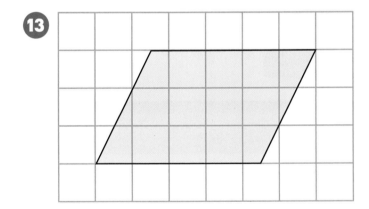

**14**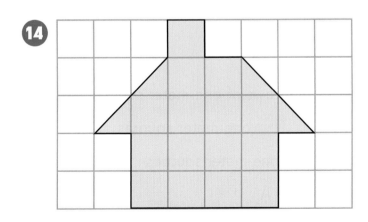

**Hands-On Activity**

Do you know what the area of your palm is?
Place your palm on a square grid.
Trace the outline of your palm.
Count the squares to estimate the area of your palm.

Material:
• square grid paper

 Count 1 square unit.

Count $\frac{1}{2}$ square unit.

 Count 1 square unit.

 Count 0 square units.

# Let's Practice

## Find the area of the figure.

**1**

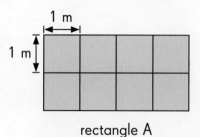

rectangle A

There are [ ] rows of one-meter squares.

Each row has [ ] one-meter squares.

There are [ ] one-meter squares

covering rectangle A.

Area of rectangle A = [ ] m$^2$

# Find the area of the figure.

**2**

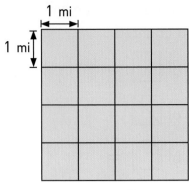

town B

Area of town B = length of side × length of side

= [ ] × [ ]

= [ ] mi²

# Find the area of each rectangle or square.

**3**

6 in.

3 in.

Area = [ ] in.²

**4**

7 cm

7 cm

Area = [ ] cm²

# Solve.

**5** The length of one side of a square window is 24 inches.
Half of the window is covered with ivy.
What area of the window is covered with ivy?

**Estimate the area of each shaded figure.**

**6**

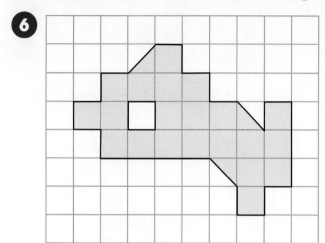

Use this to help you remember what you counted.

Number of ▢ = ⬜

Number of ◹ = ⬜

Number of ◰ = ⬜

Number of ◱ = ⬜

The area of the figure is ⬜ square units.

**7**

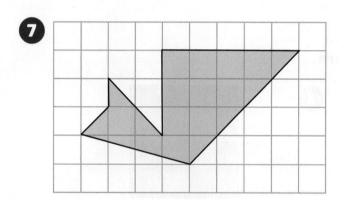

Use this to help you remember what you counted.

Number of ▢ = ⬜

Number of ◹ = ⬜

Number of ◰ = ⬜

Number of ◱ = ⬜

The area of the figure is ⬜ square units.

**ON YOUR OWN**

**Go to Workbook B:**
**Practice 1, pages 133–138**

# 13.2 Rectangles and Squares

## Lesson Objective

- Solve problems involving the area and perimeter of squares and rectangles.

### Learn Find the perimeter of a rectangle using a formula.

length

width

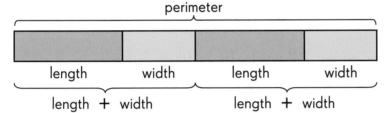

Perimeter of rectangle = length + width + length + width
= total length of all four sides

You can use a model to show that the perimeter of the rectangle is the sum of its two lengths and two widths.

perimeter

| length | width | length | width |

length + width          length + width

So, the length + width of a rectangle is equal to $\frac{1}{2}$ of its perimeter.

### Learn Find one side of a rectangle given its perimeter and the other side.

The perimeter of rectangle A is 18 feet.
Its length is 6 feet. Find its width.

Length + width = perimeter ÷ 2
= 18 ÷ 2
= 9 ft

Length + width = 9 ft
6 + width = 9 ft
width = 9 − 6
= 3 ft

The width of rectangle A is 3 feet.

6 ft

?

rectangle A

## Guided Learning

**Solve.**

**1** The perimeter of rectangle B is 28 yards.
Its length is 8 yards. Find its width.

Length $+$ width $=$ perimeter $\div$ 2

$$= \boxed{\phantom{00}} \div \boxed{\phantom{00}}$$

$$= \boxed{\phantom{00}} \text{ yd}$$

$$8 + \text{width} = \boxed{\phantom{00}} \text{ yd}$$

$$\text{width} = \boxed{\phantom{00}} - \boxed{\phantom{00}}$$

$$= \boxed{\phantom{00}} \text{ yd}$$

The width of rectangle B is $\boxed{\phantom{00}}$ yards.

8 yd

?

rectangle B

**2** The perimeter of a rectangular pool is 32 yards. Its width is 5 yards.
Find the length of the pool.

?

5 yd

**Learn** **Find one side of a square given its perimeter.**

The perimeter of a square is 64 meters.
Find the length of a side of the square.

All the sides of a square are equal.
There are 4 sides in a square.

Length of a side $=$ perimeter $\div$ 4

$$= 64 \div 4$$

$$= 16 \text{ m}$$

The length of a side of the square is 16 meters.

? m

## Guided Learning

**Solve.**

**3** Linda bent a wire 132 centimeters long into a square.
What is the length of a side of the square?

Length of a side = [    ] ÷ 4

                = [    ] cm

The length of a side of the square is [    ] centimeters.

**4** The perimeter of a square gymnasium is 36 yards.

Find the length of one side of the gymnasium.

? yd

# Let's Practice

**Solve.**

**1** The perimeter of a rectangular garden
is 128 feet. Its length is 35 feet.
Find the width of the garden.

35 ft

?

**2** Jung glued a 72-centimeter piece of decorative
string around the outer edge of a square-topped box.
What is the length of one side of the square top?

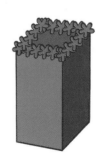

**3** Colin walked once around a rectangular field
for a total distance of 480 meters.
The length of the field is 160 meters.
What is the width of the field?

**ON YOUR OWN**

**Go to Workbook B:
Practice 2, pages 139–142**

**Find the area of a rectangle using a formula.**

Area of rectangle = length × width

In the rectangle, area = 5 × 3

$$= 15 \text{ unit}^2.$$

The area of the rectangle is 15 square units.

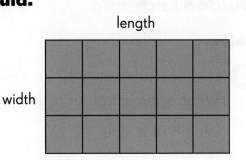

**Find one side of a rectangle given its area and the other side.**

The area of a rectangular carpet is 63 square meters.
Its length is 9 meters. Find its width.

Length × width = area

9 × width = 63 m²

Width = 63 ÷ 9

$$= 7 \text{ m}$$

The width of the rectangular carpet is 7 meters.

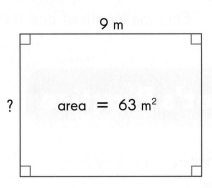

## Guided Learning

**Solve. Show your work.**

**5** The area of a rectangular piece of land is 96 square yards.
Its width is 8 yards. Find its length.

Length × [ ] = [ ] yd

Length = [ ] ÷ [ ]

= [ ] yd

The length of the rectangular piece of land is [ ] yards.

**Find one side and the perimeter of a square given its area.**

The area of square G is 25 square centimeters.

**a** Find the length of a side of the square.

$$\text{Area} = \text{length of side} \times \text{length of side}$$
$$25 = 5 \times 5$$
$$\text{Length of side} = 5 \text{ cm}$$

The length of a side of square G is 5 centimeters.

area = 25 cm²

square G

**b** Find the perimeter of the square.

$$\begin{aligned}\text{Perimeter} &= 4 \times \text{length of side} \\ &= 4 \times 5 \\ &= 20 \text{ cm}\end{aligned}$$

The perimeter of square G is 20 centimeters.

## Guided Learning

## Solve. Show your work.

**6** The area of square H is 49 square inches.

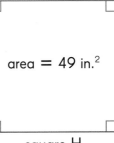

area = 49 in.²

square H

**a** Find the length of a side of the square.

Area $= 49$ in.²

$49 =$ ⬚ $\times$ ⬚

Length of side $=$ ⬚ in.

The length of a side of square H

is ⬚ inches.

> Use mental math to find a number that when multiplied by itself is 49.

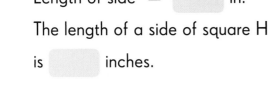

**b** Find the perimeter of the square.

Perimeter $= 4 \times$ ⬚

$=$ ⬚ in.

The perimeter of square H is ⬚ inches.

## Let's Explore!

**WORKING TOGETHER**

Materials:
- geoboard
- rubber bands
- one-inch dot paper

Work in groups of four.
Use rubber bands to make as many different rectangles
as possible on the geoboard.
Make sure that all the rectangles you make have the same perimeter.
Use dot paper to record your figures.
Record the data about the rectangles in a table like the one below.

## Example

| Rectangle | Length | Width | Perimeter | Area |
|-----------|--------|-------|-----------|------|
| A | 3 in. | 3 in. | 12 in. | 9 in.² |
| B | 4 in. | 2 in. | 12 in. | 8 in.² |

What do you notice about the area of these rectangles?

# Let's Practice

**Solve.**

**1** The area of a rectangular garden is 48 square meters. Its length is 8 meters. Find its width.

**2** The area of a square plate is 81 cm². Find the length of a side of the square plate.

? cm | area = 81 cm²

**3** The area of a rectangular office is 108 square feet. Its width is 9 feet.

**a** Find its length.

**b** Find the perimeter of the office.

**4** The area of a square kitchen is 16 m².

**a** Find the length of a side of the kitchen.

**b** Find the perimeter of the kitchen.

**5** The perimeter of a square garden is 24 yards.

**a** Find the length of its side.

**b** Find the area of the garden.

**6** The perimeter of a rectangular land preserve is 36 miles. Its length is twice the width.

**a** Find the length and width of the land preserve.

**b** Find the area of the land preserve.

**ON YOUR OWN**

**Go to Workbook B:
Practice 3, pages 143–146**

# 13.3 Composite Figures

## Lesson Objective

- Find the perimeter and area of a composite figure.

**Vocabulary**
composite figure

### Learn Find the perimeter of a **composite figure** by adding the lengths of its sides.

A composite figure is made up of different shapes.

A homeowner wants to fence in this piece of land. He draws a diagram and labels it *ABCDEF*. Find *CD* and *AF*.

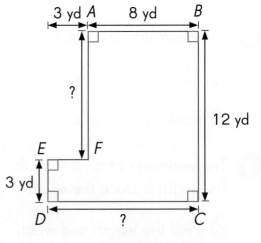

$CD = EF + AB$
$\quad = 3 + 8$
$\quad = 11$ yd

$AF = BC - DE$
$\quad = 12 - 3$
$\quad = 9$ yd

Perimeter of $ABCDEF = AB + BC + CD + DE + EF + AF$
$\qquad = 8 + 12 + 11 + 3 + 3 + 9$
$\qquad = 46$ yd

The perimeter of *ABCDEF* is 46 yards.

## Guided Learning

**Solve. Show your work.**

**1** Find the perimeter of figure *ABCDEF*.

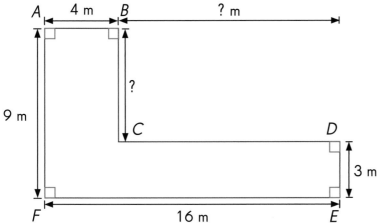

First, find *BC* and *CD*.

$BC = AF - DE$          $CD = \boxed{\phantom{xx}} - \boxed{\phantom{xx}}$

$\phantom{BC} = \boxed{\phantom{xx}} - \boxed{\phantom{xx}}$          $\phantom{CD} = \boxed{\phantom{xx}} - \boxed{\phantom{xx}}$

$\phantom{BC} = \boxed{\phantom{xx}}$ m          $\phantom{CD} = \boxed{\phantom{xx}}$ m

Perimeter of figure *ABCDEF*

$= AB + \boxed{\phantom{xx}} + \boxed{\phantom{xx}} + \boxed{\phantom{xx}} + \boxed{\phantom{xx}} + \boxed{\phantom{xx}}$

$= \boxed{\phantom{xx}} + \boxed{\phantom{xx}} + \boxed{\phantom{xx}} + \boxed{\phantom{xx}} + \boxed{\phantom{xx}} + \boxed{\phantom{xx}}$

$= \boxed{\phantom{xx}}$ m

## Find the perimeter of each figure.

**2**

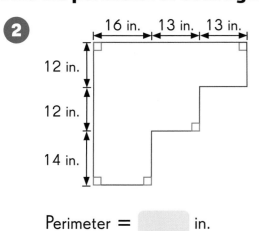

Perimeter = $\boxed{\phantom{xx}}$ in.

**3**

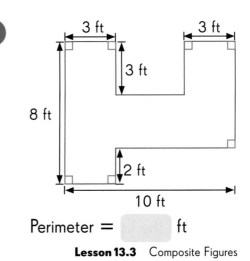

Perimeter = $\boxed{\phantom{xx}}$ ft

<sup>Learn</sup> **Find the area of a composite figure by adding the area of its parts.**

Find the area of the figure.

This figure is made up of two rectangles.
It is a composite figure.

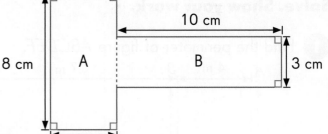

8 cm

A

10 cm

B

3 cm

4 cm

Area of a rectangle = length × width
Area of rectangle A = 8 × 4 = 32 cm²
Area of rectangle B = 10 × 3 = 30 cm²
Area of the figure = area of rectangle A + area of rectangle B
$\qquad$ = 32 + 30
$\qquad$ = 62 cm²
The area of the figure is 62 square centimeters.

## Guided Learning

## Solve.

**4** Find the area of the figure.
It is made up of a square and a rectangle.

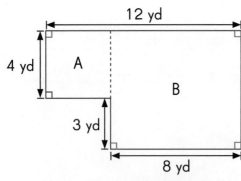

12 yd

4 yd

A

3 yd

B

8 yd

You can also divide the figure into two rectangles like this.

X
Y

How do you find the area now?

Area of square A = ◻ × ◻

$\qquad$ = ◻ yd²

Area of rectangle B = ◻ × ◻

$\qquad$ = ◻ yd²

Area of the figure = ◻ + ◻ = ◻ yd²

The area of the figure is ◻ square yards.

# Find the area of each figure.

**5**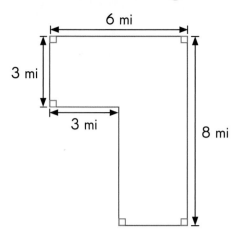

Area = [   ] mi²

**6**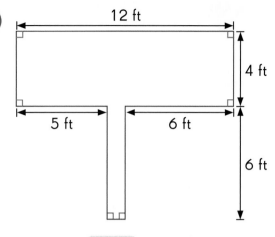

Area = [   ] ft²

**7**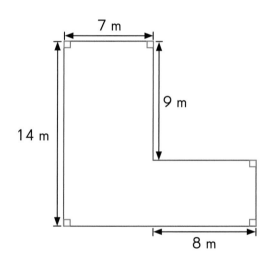

Area = [   ] m²

**8**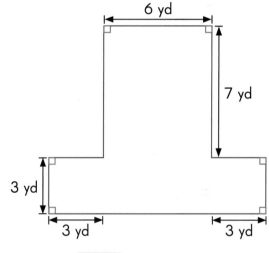

Area = [   ] yd²

**9**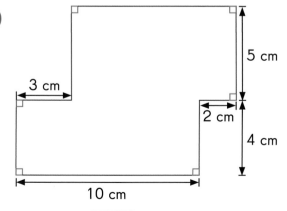

Area = [   ] cm²

# Hands-On Activity

**WORK IN PAIRS**

**STEP 1** Draw two rectangles on a sheet of square grid paper and cut them out.

**STEP 2** Draw one rectangle and one square on another sheet of square grid paper and cut them out.

**STEP 3** Draw two rectangles and one square on a third sheet of square grid paper and cut them out.

**STEP 4** Form as many different composite figures as you can using each set of cutouts.

## Example

set 1                    set 2                    set 3

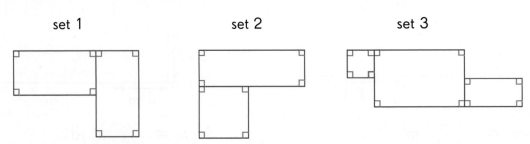

**STEP 5** Draw the figures formed on another sheet of square grid paper. Compare your figures with those of your classmates.

**STEP 6** Find the perimeter and area of each figure you have formed.

You may also use a computer tool to draw and combine squares and rectangles.

**Tech Connection**

## Let's Practice

**Find the perimeter and area of each composite figure.**

**1**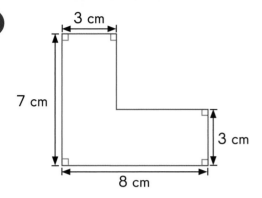

Perimeter = [　　] cm

Area = [　　] cm²

**2**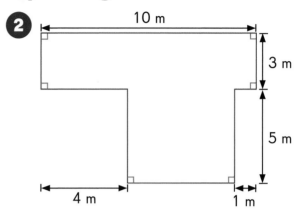

Perimeter = [　　] m

Area = [　　] m²

**3**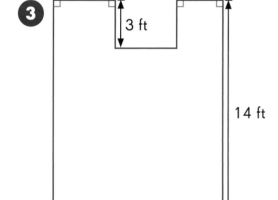

Perimeter = [　　] ft

Area = [　　] ft²

**4**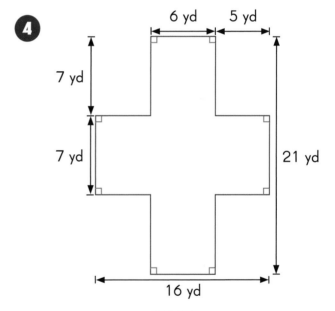

Perimeter = [　　] yd

Area = [　　] yd²

**ON YOUR OWN**

**Go to Workbook B:**
Practice 4, pages 147–150

# Lesson 13.4 Using Formulas for Area and Perimeter

## Lesson Objectives

- Solve word problems involving estimating area of figures.
- Solve word problems involving area and perimeter of composite figures.

---

**Learn Use length and width to find the area of a rectangle.**

Randy bought a diary for his brother.
What is the area of its cover page?

Randy can find the area by measuring the length and width of the cover page.

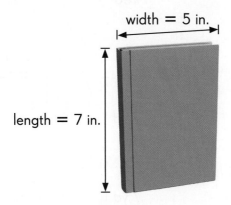

width = 5 in.

length = 7 in.

**Step 1** Length of cover page = 7 in.

**Step 2** Width of cover page = 5 in.

**Step 3** Area of cover page = length × width
= 7 × 5
= 35 in.$^2$

The area of the cover page is 35 square inches.

**Learn** **Use squares to estimate the area of a figure.**

Twyla is building a model of a park.
She wants to know how large the model of the pond is.

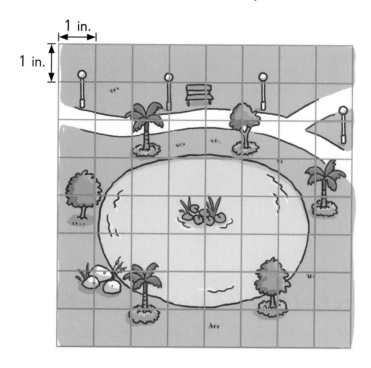

Help her estimate the area of the model.

| | | | |
|---|---|---|---|
| □ Count 1 square unit. | ◩ Count $\frac{1}{2}$ square unit. | ⬕ Count 1 square unit. | ◪ Count 0 square units. |

**Step 1** Count the □.
There are 10 □.

**Step 2** Count the ◩.
There are no ◩.

**Step 3** Count the ⬕.
There are 10 ⬕.

**Step 4** Add the squares.

10 + 10 = 20

The area of the model of the pond is about 20 square inches.

# Guided Learning

**Solve.**

**1** Find the area of the photo frame.

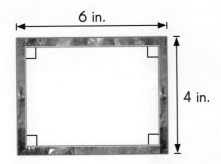

6 in.

4 in.

Area = [          ] in.²

**2** Estimate the area of the CD.

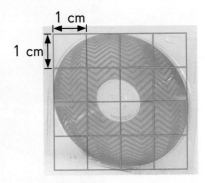

1 cm

1 cm

Estimated area = [          ] cm²

**Learn** **Use subtraction to find the area of a composite figure.**

The figure shows a small rectangle *BCDG* and a large rectangle *ACEF*.
Find the area of the shaded part of the figure.

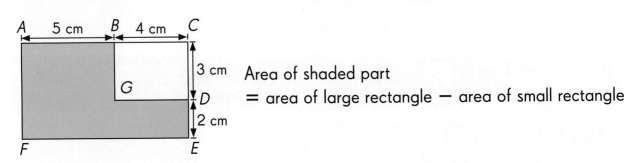

A    5 cm    B    4 cm    C

3 cm

G

D

2 cm

F                              E

Area of shaded part
= area of large rectangle − area of small rectangle

Length of large rectangle = *AC*
                          = 5 + 4 = 9 cm
Width of large rectangle = *CE*
                         = 3 + 2 = 5 cm
Area of large rectangle = 9 × 5
                        = 45 cm²
Area of small rectangle = 4 × 3
                        = 12 cm²
Area of shaded part = 45 − 12
                    = 33 cm²

The area of the shaded part is 33 square centimeters.

# Guided Learning

## Solve. Show your work.

**3** The figure shows a small rectangle *BCGH* and a large rectangle *ADEF*. Find the area of the shaded part of the figure.

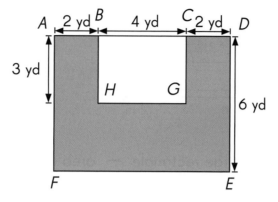

Length of large rectangle = ⬚ + ⬚ + ⬚

= ⬚ yd

Width of large rectangle = ⬚ yd

Area of large rectangle = ⬚ × ⬚

= ⬚ yd²

Area of small rectangle = ⬚ × ⬚

= ⬚ yd²

Area of shaded part = ⬚ − ⬚

= ⬚ yd²

The area of the shaded part is 36 square yards.

First, find the area of the large rectangle.

## Learn Find the area of a path around a rectangle.

The figure shows a rectangular field with a path 2 meters wide around it.
Find the area of the path.

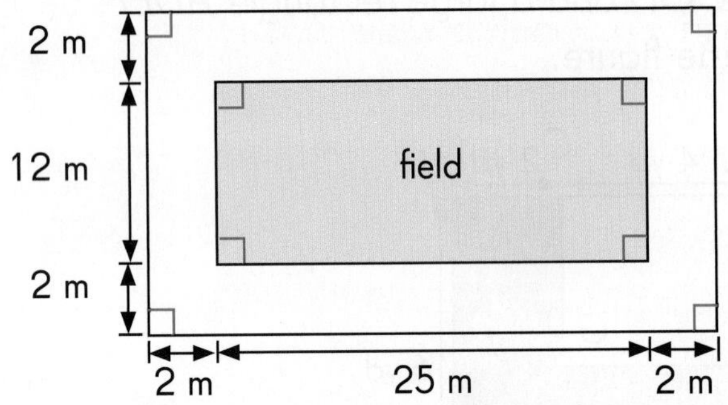


Area of path = area of large rectangle − area of small rectangle

Length of large rectangle = 2 + 25 + 2
= 29 m

Width of large rectangle = 2 + 12 + 2
= 16 m

Area of large rectangle = 29 × 16
= 464 $m^2$

Area of small rectangle = 25 × 12
= 300 $m^2$

Area of path = 464 − 300
= 164 $m^2$

The area of the path is 164 square meters.

# Guided Learning

## Solve. Show your work.

**4** A rectangular piece of fabric measures 80 inches by 60 inches.
When placed on a table, it leaves a margin 5 inches wide all around it.
Find the area of the table not covered by the fabric.

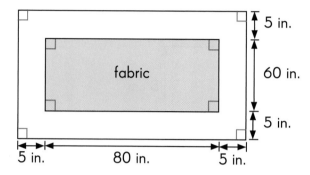

Area of table not covered by fabric = area of table − area of fabric

Length of table = [    ] + [    ] + [    ]

= [    ] in.

Width of table = [    ] + [    ] + [    ]

= [    ] in.

Area of table = [    ] × [    ]

= [    ] in.$^2$

Area of fabric = [    ] × [    ]

= [    ] in.$^2$

Area of table not covered by fabric = [    ] − [    ]

= [    ] in.$^2$

The area of the table not covered by the fabric is [    ] square inches.

## Solve.

**5** Ryan has a rectangular sheet of paper with a length of 13 centimeters and a width of 8 centimeters. He cuts away a small rectangle at one of its corners. The length and width of the small rectangle are shown in the figure.

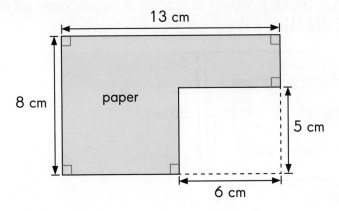

**a** Find the remaining area of the paper.

**b** Find the perimeter of the remaining paper.

**6** There is a 1.5-yard wide path around a rectangular piece of land. The length and width of the path are shown in the figure.

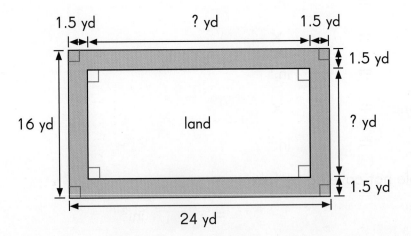

**a** Find the area of the land.

**b** Find the perimeter of the land.

## Learn **Find the area and perimeter of parts of a figure.**

A corner of a square piece of paper is folded.

**a** Find the area of the shaded part.

The shaded part is half of a 2-inch square.

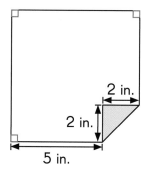

Area of 2-inch square $= 2 \times 2$
$$= 4 \text{ in.}^2$$
So, area of shaded part $= 4 \div 2$
$$= 2 \text{ in.}^2$$
The area of the shaded part is 2 square inches.

**b** Find the perimeter of the square piece of paper unfolded.

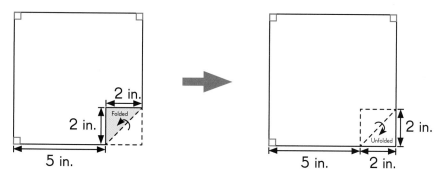

To find the perimeter of the square piece of paper unfolded,
you need to find the length of a side of the square.
Length of a side $= 5 + 2$
$$= 7 \text{ in.}$$
Perimeter of the square $= 4 \times 7$
$$= 28 \text{ in.}$$
The perimeter of the square piece of paper is 28 inches.

# Guided Learning

**Solve.**

**7** A rectangular piece of paper is folded at one of its corners so that the side *BC* lies along the side *CD* as shown.

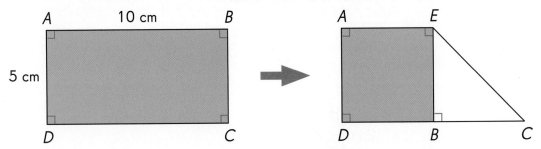

**a** Find the area of the rectangular piece of paper before it was folded.

**b** Find the area of the figure after the paper was folded.

 **Hands-On Activity**

Material:
* centimeter square grid paper

STEP
**1** Draw a shape like this on square grid paper.

STEP
**2** Estimate the area of the shape.

STEP
**3** Draw the largest possible rectangle within the shape along the grid lines. Use the square grid to help you.

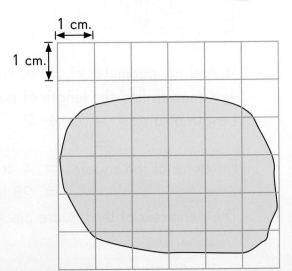

# Let's Explore!

**Material:**
- centimeter square grid paper

**STEP 1** Draw a rectangle with a length of 8 centimeters and a width of 6 centimeters on the centimeter grid paper.

**STEP 2** Label the length and width. Find the area.

**STEP 3** Cut out the rectangle.

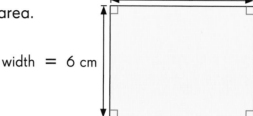

length = 8 cm

width = 6 cm

**STEP 4** Fold the cut-out rectangle to make a rectangle of a different size. Measure the length and width of this shape. Then, find the area.

**Example**

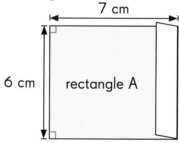

7 cm

6 cm    rectangle A

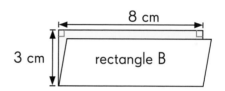

8 cm

3 cm    rectangle B

**STEP 5** Unfold the rectangle you made in **STEP 4**. Fold it to make another rectangular shape. This time take only one measurement — measure the side that is changed by the folding. Then, find the area of the folded rectangle.

**STEP 6** Check your answer by measuring the length and width of the folded rectangle.

**STEP 7** Make two more rectangles with the cutout. Take only one measurement for each rectangle as in **STEP 5**.

Then, find its area. Does your method of using one measurement to find the area apply for these rectangles too?

**Solve.**

**1** The perimeter of a rectangular garden is 60 feet.
The width of a picket fence around the garden is 12 feet.
Find its length.

**2** The filled figure is made up of 2-inch squares. Find the shaded area.

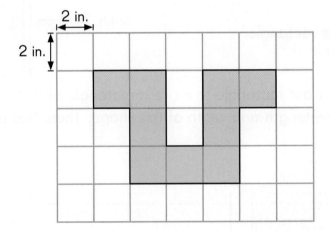

**3** Cory spilled purple paint all over his grid paper.
Estimate the area covered by the paint.

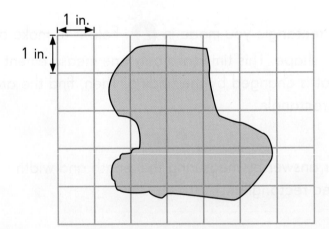

# Solve.

**4** The area below shows the cattleyard of a farmer.
Find the length of the cattle fence around the perimeter of the yard.

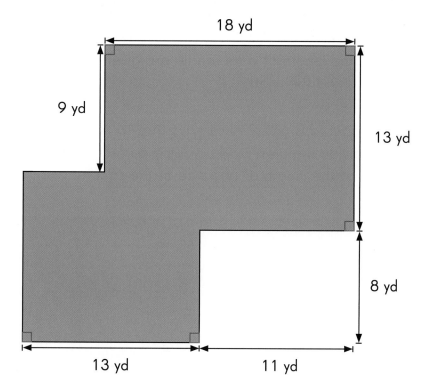

**5** Lionel is laying a carpet on the floor of a rectangular room.
The border around the carpet is 1 meter wide.
How much space is not covered by the carpet?

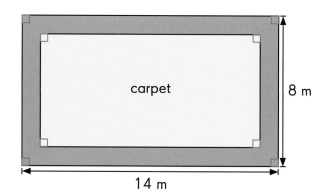

**ON YOUR OWN**

**Go to Workbook B:**
**Practice 5, pages 151–156**

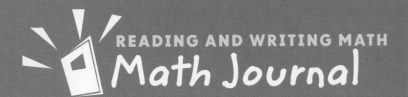

## READING AND WRITING MATH
# Math Journal

1. The perimeter and length of a rectangle are given.
   List the steps to find the width.

2. The area of a square is given. Alice says that to find the length of one side, she can divide the area by 4. Is Alice correct? If not, explain to Alice how to find the length of one side of the square.

## CRITICAL THINKING SKILLS
# Put On Your Thinking Cap!

### PROBLEM SOLVING

1. What is the length of one side of a square if its perimeter and area have the same numerical value?

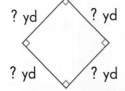

? yd   ? yd
? yd   ? yd

Make an organized list.

2. A rectangular piece of paper has a length of 12 inches and a width of 8 inches. What is the greatest number of 3-inch by 3-inch squares that can be drawn on the piece of paper, without overlapping?

**PROBLEM SOLVING**

**3** Study the figure. All line segments meet at right angles.
What is the perimeter of the figure? Explain your reasoning.

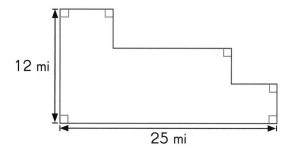

12 mi

25 mi

**4** Vicky arranged two different square pieces of paper as shown.
The length of one side of each square piece of paper is a whole number.

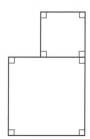

The total area of the figure is 89 square centimeters.
What is the length of the side of each square piece of paper?
On a piece of paper, copy and complete the table below.

| Length of the Square (cm) | 1 | 2 | 3 | 4 | 5 | 6 | 7 | 8 | 9 | 10 |
|---|---|---|---|---|---|---|---|---|---|---|
| Area of the Square (cm²) | 1 | 4 | 9 | | | | | | | |

Use the data in the table to find the areas of the two squares
that have a sum of 89 square centimeters.

ON YOUR OWN

**Go to Workbook B:
Put On Your Thinking Cap!
pages 157–162**

# Chapter Wrap Up

## Study Guide

**You have learned...**

**BIG IDEA**

▶ Area and perimeter of a square, rectangle, or composite figure can be found by counting squares or using a formula.

**Perimeter**

**Area**

### Distance Around a Figure

Find the perimeter of a rectangle or square.
- Length + width + length + width

Use these units: cm, m, in., ft, yd, mi

### Amount of Surface Covered

Find the area of a rectangle or square.
- Counting unit squares
- Length × width

Use these units: $cm^2$, $m^2$, $in.^2$, $ft^2$, $yd^2$, $mi^2$

Find the length of one side of a rectangle given the perimeter and the other side.

Length + width = perimeter ÷ 2

Find the length of one side of a square given the perimeter.

Length of one side = perimeter ÷ 4

Find the area of a rectangle using the formula.

Length × width = area

Find the length of the sides of a square given the area.

Length of side × length of side = area

Find the length of one side of a rectangle given the area and the other side.

Length = area ÷ width

## Composite Figures

### Find Area

Divide the composite figure into rectangle(s) and/or square(s) to find the area.

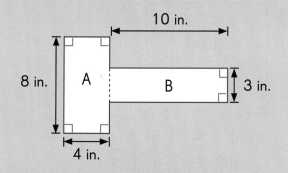

Area of rectangle A  = 8 × 4
                       = 32 in.²
Area of rectangle B  = 10 × 3
                       = 30 in.²
Area of figure  = 32 + 30
                 = 62 in.²

### Find Perimeter

First, find the unknown lengths. Then find the perimeter.

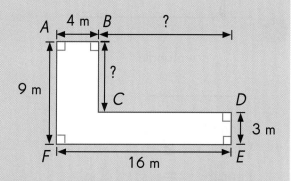

Perimeter
= 9 + 4 + 6 + 12 + 3 + 16
= 50 m

# Chapter Review/Test

## Vocabulary

### Choose the correct word.

> composite figure
>
> length
>
> width

**1** The longer side of a rectangle is usually called

its [＿＿＿] and the shorter side is called its [＿＿＿].

**2** A figure made up of squares and rectangles is an example of

a [＿＿＿].

## Concepts and Skills

### Find the missing lengths of the sides of each figure.

**3**

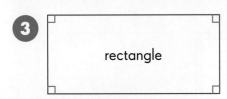

Perimeter  =  32 in.
Width     =  5 in.
Length    =  [＿＿＿] in.

**4**

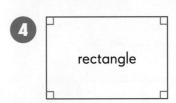

Area    =  96 m²
Width   =  8 m
Length  =  [＿＿＿] m

**5**

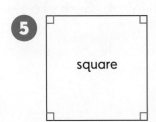

Perimeter  =  28 yd
Length of one side  =  [＿＿＿] yd

**6**

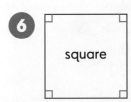

Area  =  49 km²
Length of one side  =  [＿＿＿] km

**7** **Find the area and perimeter of the figure.**

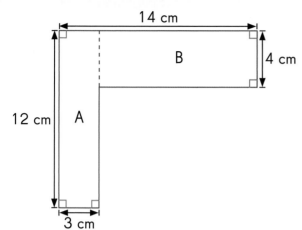

Area      =  ▢ cm²

Perimeter =  ▢ cm

## Problem Solving

### Estimate the area of each figure.

**8**

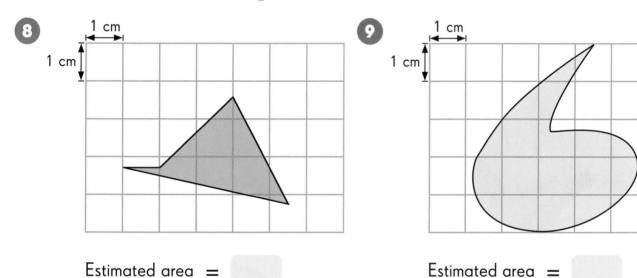

Estimated area = ▢

**9**

Estimated area = ▢

## Solve.

**10** The figure shows a rectangular grass plot of land with a path through its center.

  **a** How much land is covered with grass?

  **b** How much fencing is needed to surround the land covered with grass?

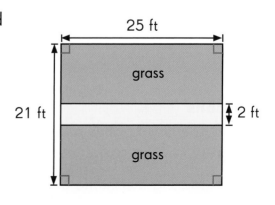

# Symmetry

## Symmetry in Nature

butterfly

scallop shell

starfish

crab

**Lessons**

**BIG IDEA**

▶ Figures can have line or rotational symmetry, or both.

# Recall Prior Knowledge

## Knowing polygons

A polygon is a closed figure formed from line segments
that meet only at their endpoints. These figures are polygons.

  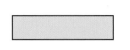  

## Identifying congruent figures

Shapes A and D have the same size and shape.
They are congruent.
Shapes B, C, and E are not congruent.

  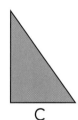 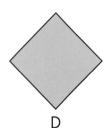 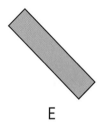

| A | B | C | D | E |

## Identifying symmetric figures

Figures A and B are symmetric.
When figures A and B are folded along the dotted lines, the two halves
match exactly. Figures C and D are not symmetric.

 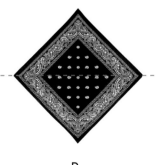  

| A | B | C | D |

## Decide which of these figures are not polygons.

**1**

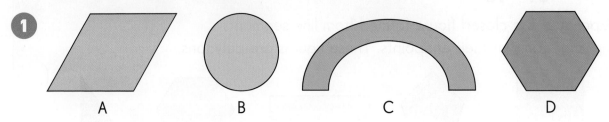

A      B      C      D

## Decide which of these pairs of shapes are congruent.

**2**

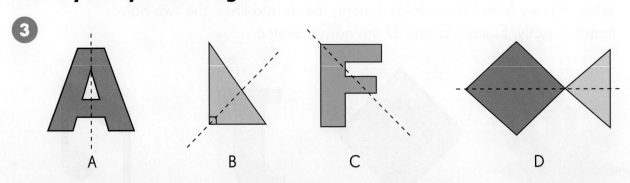

A    B    C    D

E    F    G    H    I

## Identify the symmetric figures.

**3**

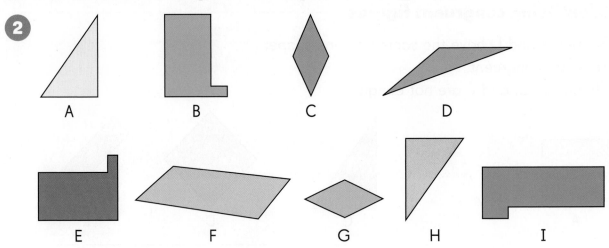

A      B      C      D

# Identifying Lines of Symmetry

## Lesson Objective

• Identify a line of symmetry of a figure.

**Vocabulary**
line of symmetry

symmetric figure

### Learn **Identify a line of symmetry of a figure.**

Fold figure A along the dotted line as shown.

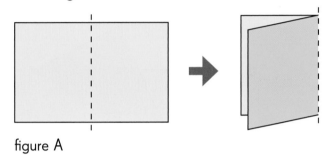

figure A

The two parts are congruent and they match exactly.

The dotted line is a **line of symmetry** of figure A.

So, figure A is a **symmetric figure** as it has line symmetry.

Now fold figure A along the dotted line as shown.

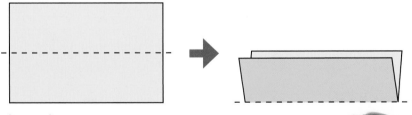

figure A

The two parts are congruent and they match exactly.

The dotted line is another line of symmetry of figure A.

A symmetric figure can have more than one line of symmetry.

Continued on next page

Now fold figure A along the line as shown.

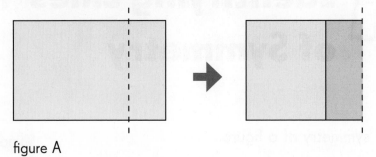

figure A

The two parts are not congruent so they do not match exactly.
The dotted line is not a line of symmetry.

Look at the two parts formed by folding along the dotted line.

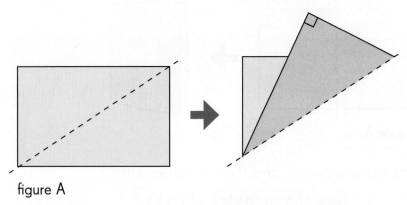

figure A

The two parts are congruent but they do not match exactly.
The dotted line is not a line of symmetry of figure A.

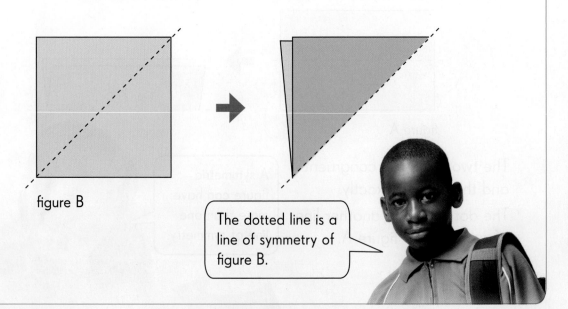

figure B

The dotted line is a line of symmetry of figure B.

## Hands-On Activity

**Materials:**
• paper
• scissors

**STEP 1** Fold a piece of paper in half.

**STEP 2** Cut out a figure that starts from a point on the fold line and ends on another point on the same fold line.

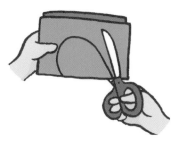

**STEP 3** Unfold your symmetric figure.

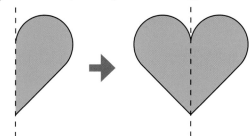

The fold line is a line of symmetry.

**STEP 4** Compare your figure with those of your classmates.

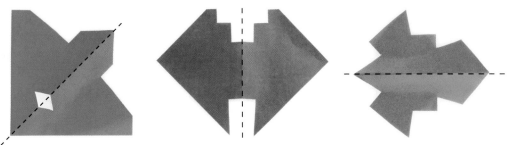

# Guided Learning

## Complete.

**1** The dotted line divides each figure into two congruent parts.

Which of the dotted lines are lines of symmetry of each hexagon?

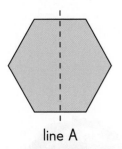

line A

Fold a copy of the hexagon along line A.

The two parts [ ] exactly.

Line A is a [ ].

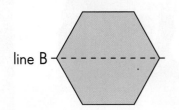

line B

Fold a copy of the hexagon along line B.

The two parts [ ] exactly.

Line B is a [ ].

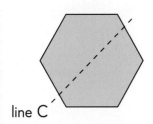

line C

Fold a copy of the hexagon along line C.

The two parts [ ] exactly.

Line C is [ ].

line D

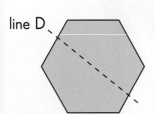

Fold a copy of the hexagon along line D.

The two parts [ ] exactly.

Line D is [ ].

# Hands-On Activity

**Materials:**
- paper
- scissors
- coloring pencils

**1** Use a sheet of paper with this shape on it.

**STEP 1** Cut out the shape.

**STEP 2** Fold the shape to get

**a** two parts that are congruent and match exactly.
Use a red coloring pencil to draw along the fold line.

**b** two parts that are congruent but do **not** match exactly.
Use a blue coloring pencil to draw along the fold line.

**c** two parts that are **not** congruent and do **not** match exactly.
Use a green coloring pencil to draw along the fold line.

Which of these lines is a line of symmetry? Explain your answer.

**2** Use a computer drawing tool to draw these figures.

*Tech Connection*

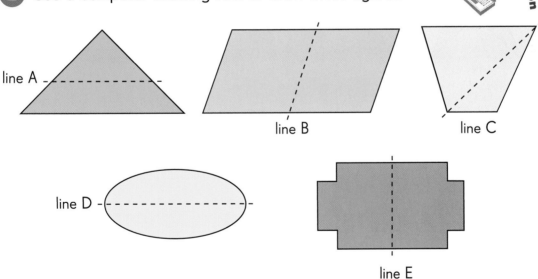

line A

line B

line C

line D

line E

Print the figures and cut them out.
Draw a dotted line on each figure as shown and fold along it.
Which of the dotted lines are lines of symmetry?

# Let's Practice

**Which of the dotted lines are lines of symmetry?**

**1**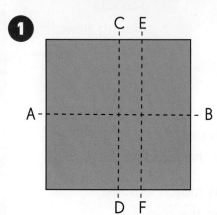

**2**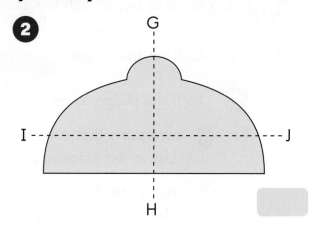

**3**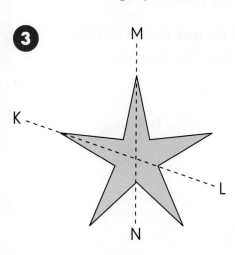

**4**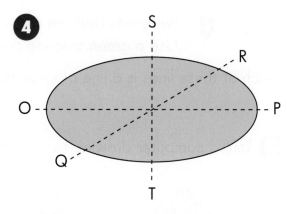

**5**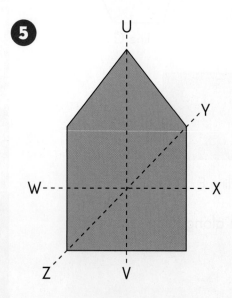

**6**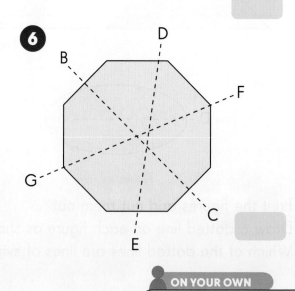

**ON YOUR OWN**

**Go to Workbook B:**
**Practice 1, pages 163–164**

# Rotational Symmetry

## Lesson Objectives

- Relate rotational symmetry to turns.
- Trace a figure to determine whether it has rotational symmetry.

| Vocabulary | |
| --- | --- |
| rotation | rotational symmetry |
| center of rotation | clockwise |
| counterclockwise | |

**Learn** **A** **rotation** **turns a figure about a point.**

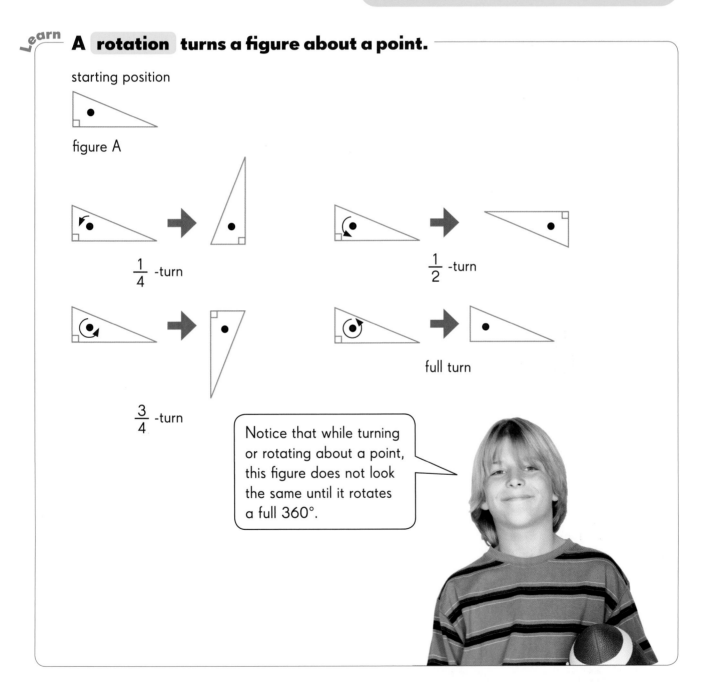

starting position

figure A

$\frac{1}{4}$ -turn

$\frac{1}{2}$ -turn

$\frac{3}{4}$ -turn

full turn

Notice that while turning or rotating about a point, this figure does not look the same until it rotates a full 360°.

Look at figure B.

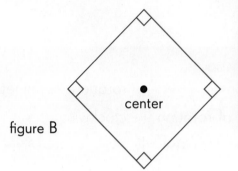

figure B

**Clockwise**: A rotation in the same direction as the hands on a clock.

**Counterclockwise**: A rotation in the opposite direction as the hands on a clock.

Figure B was rotated counterclockwise about its **center of rotation** through a

**a** $\frac{1}{4}$ -turn (90°):

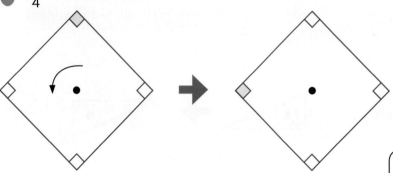

**b** $\frac{1}{2}$ -turn (180°):

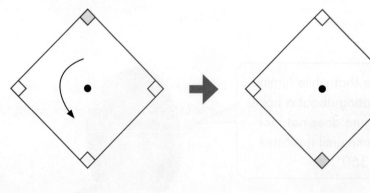

At $\frac{1}{4}$ -turn and $\frac{1}{2}$ -turn, figure B looks the same as it did before the turn.

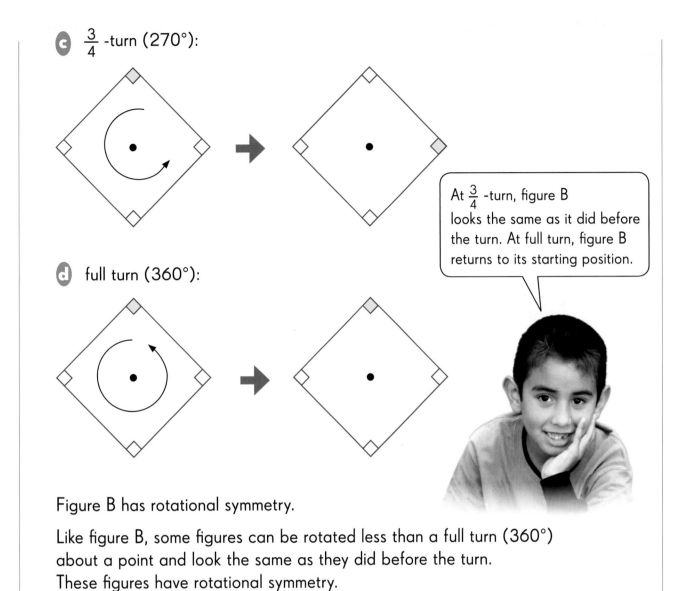

**c** $\frac{3}{4}$ -turn (270°):

**d** full turn (360°):

At $\frac{3}{4}$ -turn, figure B looks the same as it did before the turn. At full turn, figure B returns to its starting position.

Figure B has rotational symmetry.

Like figure B, some figures can be rotated less than a full turn (360°) about a point and look the same as they did before the turn. These figures have rotational symmetry.

## Guided Learning

### Decide whether the figure has rotational symmetry. Explain your answer.

**1** Figure A

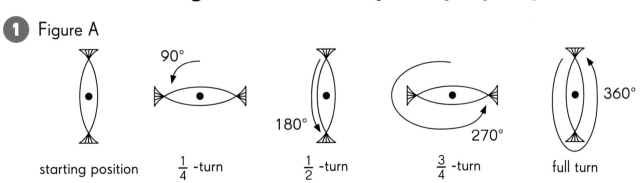

starting position     $\frac{1}{4}$ -turn     $\frac{1}{2}$ -turn     $\frac{3}{4}$ -turn     full turn

**Decide whether the figure has rotational symmetry. Explain your answer.**

2  Figure B

    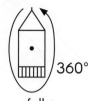

              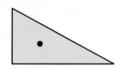

starting position     $\frac{1}{4}$ -turn     $\frac{1}{2}$ -turn     $\frac{3}{4}$ -turn     full turn

**Decide which figures have rotational symmetry. Explain your answer. Trace each figure to check.**

3

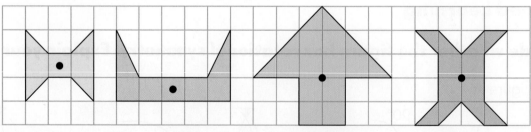

**Hands-On Activity**

**WORK IN PAIRS**

Materials:
• grid paper
• pencil

STEP
**1**  Draw one of these shapes on grid paper.

figure A      figure B      figure C      figure D

STEP
**2**  Your partner traces your drawing on another piece of grid paper, places a pencil tip in the center of the figure, and rotates it.

STEP
**3**  Decide whether the figure has rotational symmetry.

**STEP**
**4** Switch roles and repeat **STEP** **1** to **STEP** **3** for the other three shapes.

**STEP**
**5** Discuss how to decide if a figure has rotational symmetry.

**STEP**
**6** Draw your own figure that has rotational symmetry.

## Let's Practice

**Decide if these figures have rotational symmetry. Use yes or no.**

**1**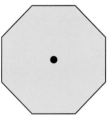

**2**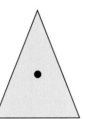

**3**

**4**

**5**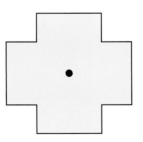

**6**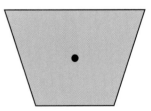

**ON YOUR OWN**

**Go to Workbook B:**
**Practice 2, pages 165–166**

# 14.3 Making Symmetric Shapes and Patterns

## Lesson Objectives

- Draw a shape or pattern about a line of symmetry and check for rotational symmetry.
- Complete a symmetric shape or pattern.
- Create symmetric patterns on grid paper.

**Learn** **Form a symmetric pattern with rotational symmetry.**

Kelly created her own symmetric pattern on grid paper.

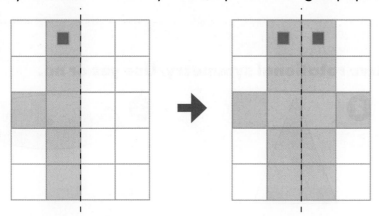

Kelly rotated the pattern through a $\frac{1}{2}$-turn (180°) about a point.

She found out that her pattern also had rotational symmetry.

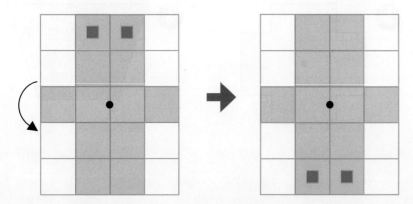

# Guided Learning

**Each figure shows half of a symmetric shape. The dotted line is a line of symmetry. Copy each figure on grid paper. Complete each symmetric shape. Decide which of these shapes have rotational symmetry.**

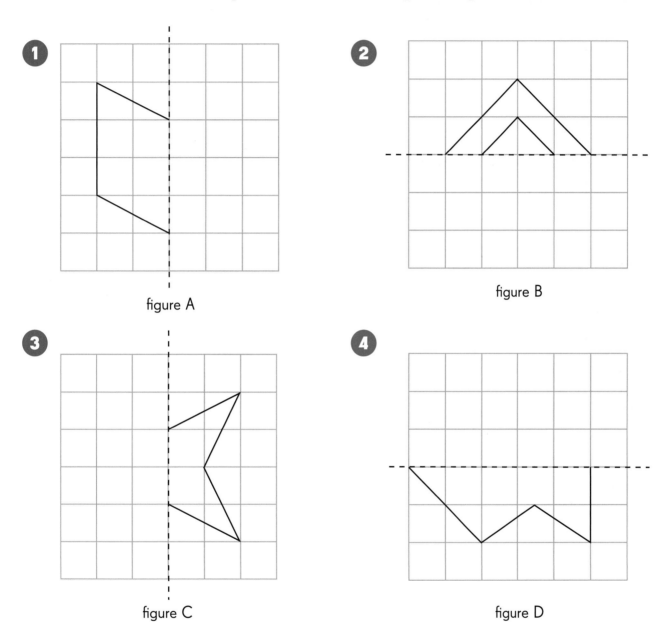

**1** figure A

**2** figure B

**3** figure C

**4** figure D

**Each figure shows half of a symmetric pattern. The dotted line is a line of symmetry. Copy each figure on grid paper. Shade the squares to form a symmetric pattern about the given line of symmetry. Decide which of these figures have rotational symmetry.**

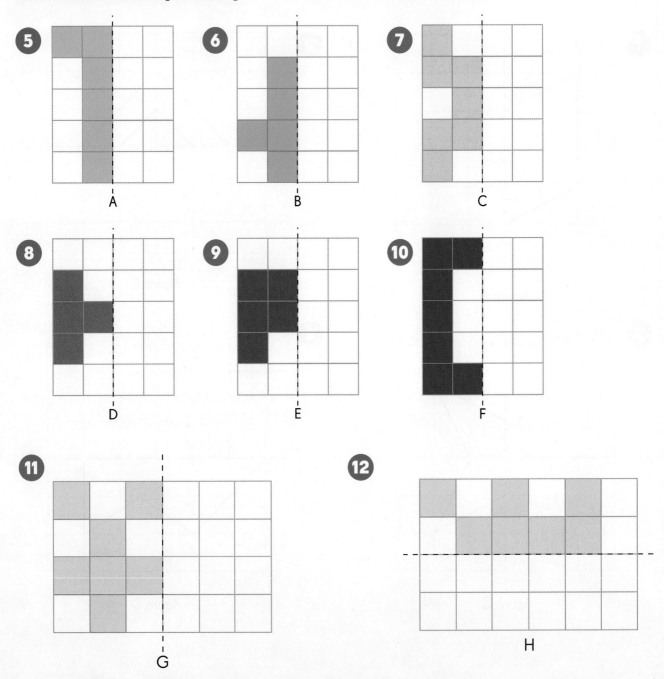

5    A

6    B

7    C

8    D

9    E

10    F

11    G

12    H

 **Hands-On Activity**

Materials:
• coloring pencil
• grid paper

**STEP 1** Divide the grid paper into halves by drawing a dotted line as shown.

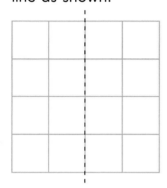

**STEP 2** Color a square on the left side of the grid paper.

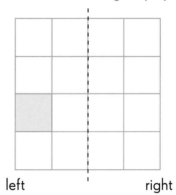

left        right

**STEP 3** Color a square on the right side of the grid paper to form a symmetric pattern.

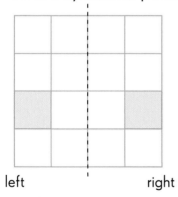

left        right

**STEP 4** Continue coloring the left side, and then the right side until you have designed your own symmetric pattern. You may color ▢ or ◺.

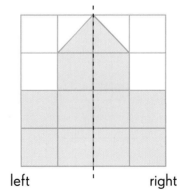

left        right

## Let's Practice

Each figure shows half of a symmetric shape or pattern. The dotted line is a line of symmetry. Copy each figure on grid paper and complete it. Decide which of these figures have rotational symmetry. Use ✔ or ✗.

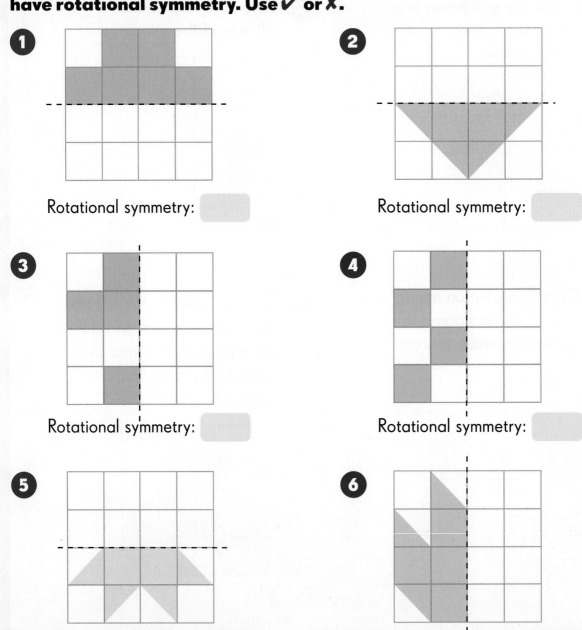

**1**

Rotational symmetry: ▢

**2**

Rotational symmetry: ▢

**3**

Rotational symmetry: ▢

**4**

Rotational symmetry: ▢

**5**

Rotational symmetry: ▢

**6**

Rotational symmetry: ▢

ON YOUR OWN

Go to Workbook B:
Practice 3, pages 167–170

# Put On Your Thinking Cap!

## PROBLEM SOLVING

**1** Which of these figures are symmetric?

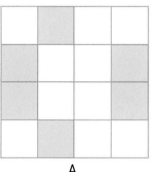

A

B

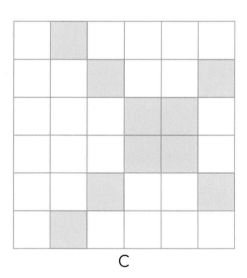

C

**2** Which figure in Exercise 1 is not symmetric?
On a sheet of grid paper, copy the figure and color
one or more squares to make it symmetric.
Does it have rotational symmetry as well?

## PROBLEM SOLVING

3 Lionel is making a pattern of symmetric figures. He has made three pieces of the pattern. Can you help Lionel to make the fourth piece? Draw it on a sheet of grid paper.

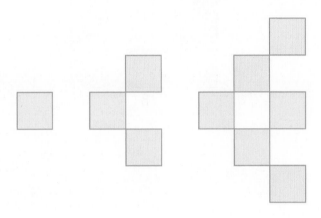

1st          2nd               3rd

ON YOUR OWN

Go to Workbook B:
Put On Your Thinking Cap!
pages 171–172

# Chapter Wrap Up

## Study Guide

### You have learned...

**Symmetry**

## Line Symmetry

To determine whether a given line is a line of symmetry of a figure.

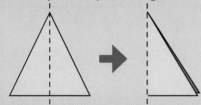

The two parts are congruent and they match exactly. So, the fold line is along a line of symmetry.

To recognize that a figure can have more than one line of symmetry.

## Rotational Symmetry

To identify a figure which has rotational symmetry about a given point. Figures can be rotated clockwise or counterclockwise about a center of rotation.

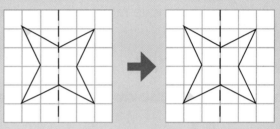

## Making Symmetric Shapes and Patterns

To complete a symmetric shape or pattern given a line of symmetry, and half of the shape or pattern. Then to check it for rotational symmetry.

Symmetric shape

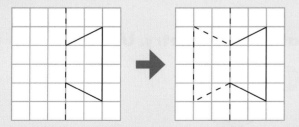

Symmetric pattern

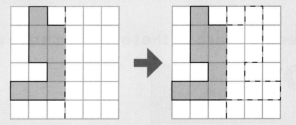

To create symmetric patterns on grid paper.

# Chapter Review/Test

## Vocabulary

### Choose the correct word.

> line symmetry
> line of symmetry
> symmetric figure
> rotation
> rotational symmetry
> center of rotation
> clockwise
> counterclockwise

**1** When a figure can be folded in half so that the two parts are congruent and match exactly, the figure has _____.

**2** A line that divides a figure into two congruent parts that match exactly is a _____.

**3** A figure that is rotated less than 360° about a point and looks the same as it did before the turn has _____.

**4** A _____ can have more than one line of symmetry.

## Concepts and Skills

### Solve. Which of the dotted lines are lines of symmetry?

**5**
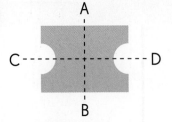

**6**
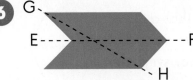

**7**
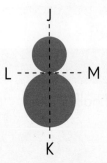

**8**
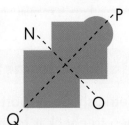

## Decide which of these figures have rotational symmetry. Use yes or no.

**9**

**10**

**Decide which of these figures have rotational symmetry. Use yes or no.**

⑪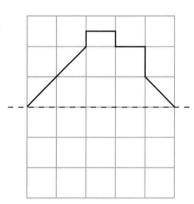

⑫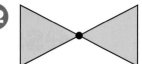

**Each figure shows half of a symmetric shape or pattern.
The dotted line is a line of symmetry of the figure. Copy each figure on grid paper and complete it. Decide which of these figures have rotational symmetry. Use ✔ or ✗.**

⑬

Rotational symmetry:

⑭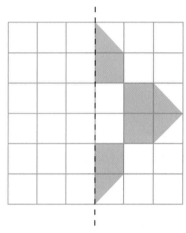

Rotational symmetry:

**Create a symmetric pattern about these lines of symmetry on grid paper.
Use only ■ and ◣.**

⑮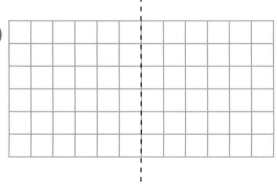

⑯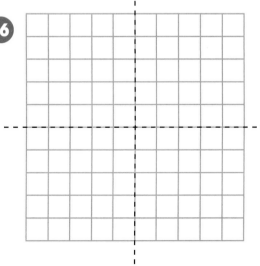

# Tessellations

## Lessons

**15.1** Identifying Tessellations

**15.2** More Tessellations

💡 **BIG IDEA**

▶ A tessellation is made when a shape (or shapes) is repeated, covering a plane (or surface) without gaps or overlaps to form patterns.

# Recall Prior Knowledge

## Drawing shapes on dot paper

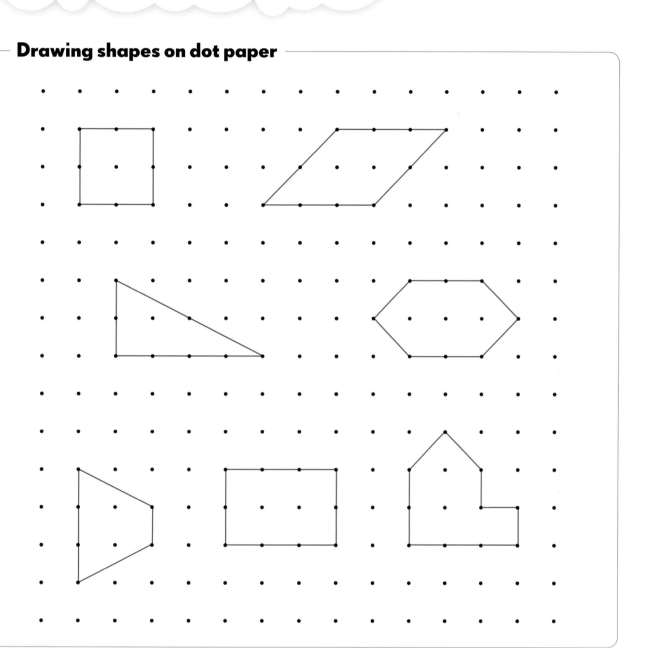

## Making patterns with shapes

## Draw these shapes on dot paper.

**1**

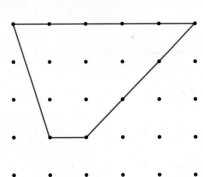

**2**

## Complete each pattern.

**3**

**4**

# Lesson 15.1 Identifying Tessellations

## Lesson Objectives

- Recognize and make tessellations.
- Identify the unit shape used in a tessellation.

**Vocabulary**

tessellation

repeated shape

slide

rotate

flip

**Learn** **Repeat shapes to make patterns.**

Look at the picture. It shows part of a floor covered with rectangular tiles.

Look at these shapes.

These shapes can be used to cover a surface with no gaps between them.

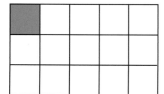 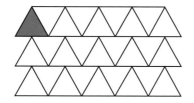 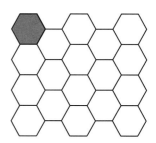

These patterns are called **tessellations**.
A tessellation can be made using a single **repeated shape**.

<sup>Learn</sup> **Some shapes do not tessellate.**

Look at these shapes.

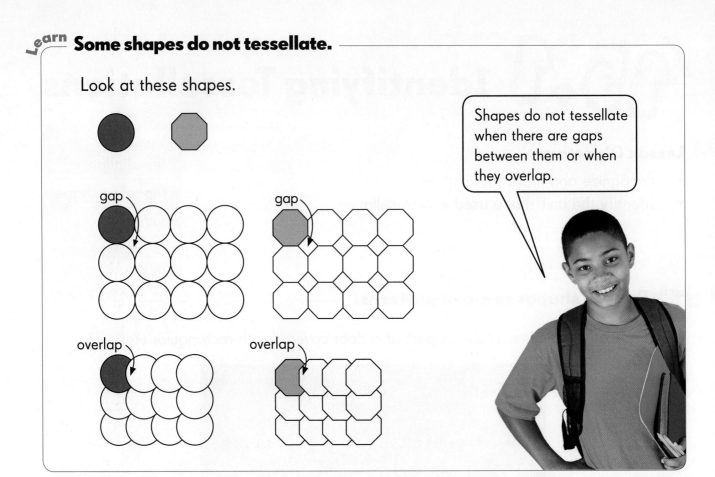

Shapes do not tessellate when there are gaps between them or when they overlap.

## Guided Learning

### Copy, identify, and color the repeated shape used in each tessellation.

**1**

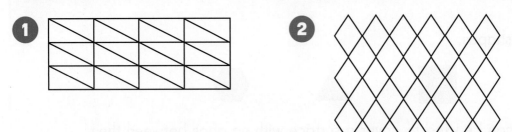

**2**

**3**

**4**

# Learn Repeat shapes to form tessellations.

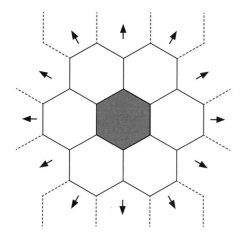

You can form a tessellation by repeating the shape in all directions.

# Learn Repeat shapes in different ways to form tessellations.

You can repeat  in several ways to form a tessellation.

**a** You can **slide** the shape.

**b** You can **rotate** the shape.

Clockwise rotation:

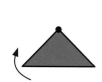   

Counterclockwise rotation:

Continued on next page

**c** You can **flip** the shape.

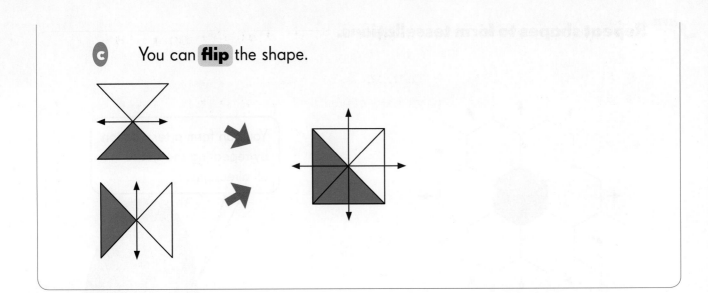

## Guided Learning

**Identify how each shape was moved. Choose slide, rotate, or flip.**

**5**

**6**

**7**

**Learn** **Repeat shapes in more ways to form tessellations.**

You can flip, then rotate the shape.

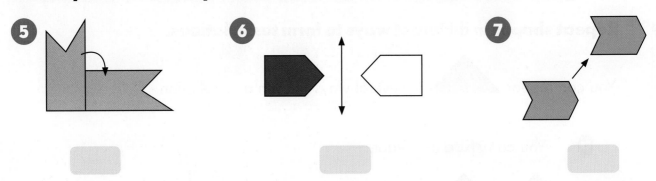

**Hands-On Activity**

**WORK IN PAIRS**

Use ten copies of each shape.

**1** Identify the shapes that tessellate.

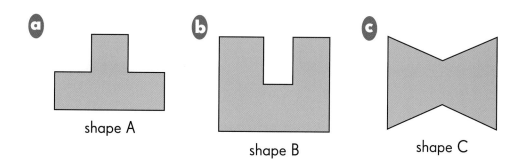

**a**

shape A

**b**

shape B

**c**

shape C

**2** Use dot paper to identify the shapes that tessellate.

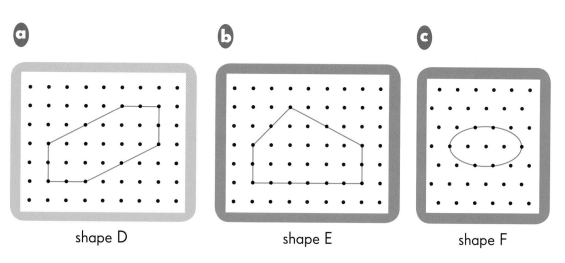

**a**

shape D

**b**

shape E

**c**

shape F

# Guided Learning

**Copy each shape on dot paper. Make a tessellation with each shape. Use slide, flip, or rotate to explain how you tessellated the shape.**

**8**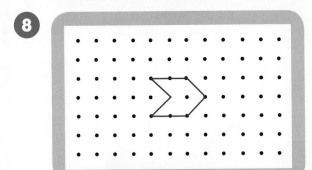

**9**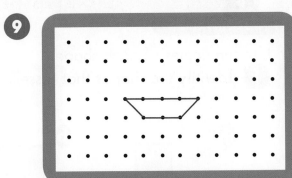

## Let's Explore!

**Tech Connection**

**WORK IN PAIRS**

**STEP 1** Use the computer drawing tool to draw a triangle and make twelve copies of the triangle.

**STEP 2** Print and cut out the triangles. Mark the angles as shown. Your triangle can be different from the one shown below.

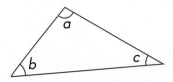

**STEP 3** Tessellate the triangles.

Can all triangles tessellate?

## Let's Practice

**Copy, identify, and color the repeated shape used in each tessellation.**

 **1**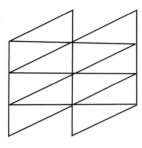

**2**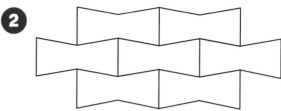

**Copy each shape on dot paper. Make a tessellation with each shape.**

**3**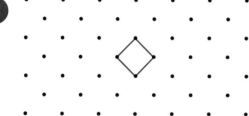

**4**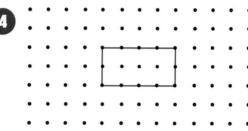

**5**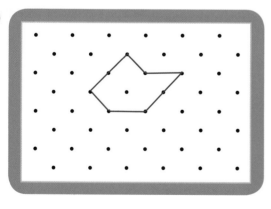

**6**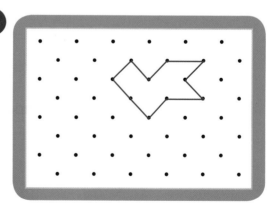

**ON YOUR OWN**

**Go to Workbook B:**
Practice 1, pages 173–178

# 15.2 More Tessellations

**Vocabulary**
modify

## Lesson Objective

- Tessellate shapes in different ways.

### Learn Tessellate shapes in different ways.

Here are some ways this shape ▭ tessellates.

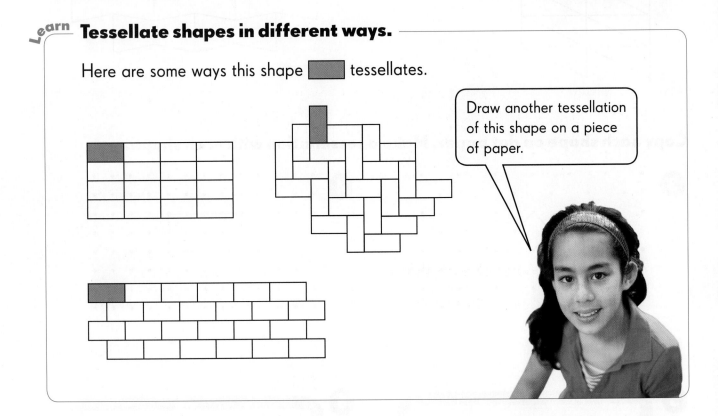

Draw another tessellation of this shape on a piece of paper.

### Learn Tessellate shapes in more ways to form different tessellations.

You can rotate, then flip the shape.

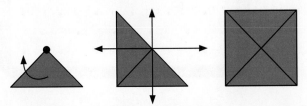

You can slide, then rotate the shape.

  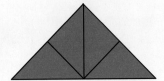

## Guided Learning

**Copy the shape on dot paper. Tessellate the shape in another way.**

**1**

---

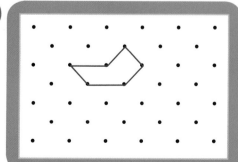

### Hands-On Activity

**Materials:**
- shape worksheet
- dot paper

**1** Use ten copies of each shape.

Tessellate each shape in two different ways.

**a**

**b**

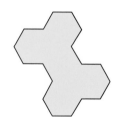

**2** Copy each shape on dot paper.

Make as many different tessellations as you can for each shape.

**a**                    **b**

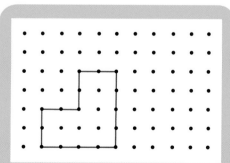

### Learn **Modify shapes to make tessellations.**

Cassie designed a pattern for an art competition. She modified a square to create the repeated shape for the tessellation.

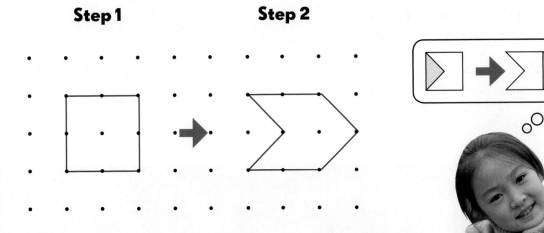

**Step 1**          **Step 2**

She cut out the shape and made copies of it. She colored half of the shapes blue and the other half of the shapes yellow. Then she repeated the shape to make a tessellation.

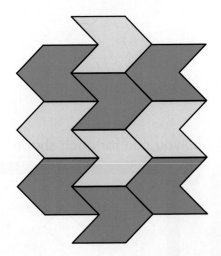

**More ways to modify shapes to make tessellations.**

Cassie decided to create a second design using a different shape.

**Step 1**     **Step 2**     **Step 3**

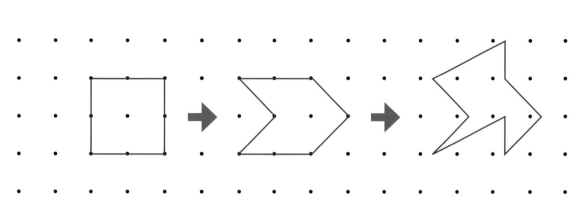

She cut out the shape and made copies of it.
Then she colored the shapes and repeated them
to make another tessellation.

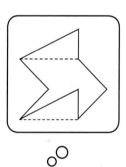

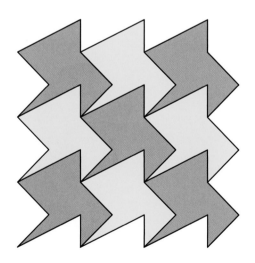

Continued on next page

Ben showed how he designed the repeated shape for his tessellation.

**Step 1**   **Step 2**   **Step 3**

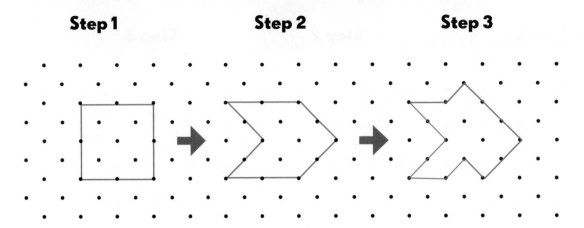

Ben repeated the shape to make his tessellation.

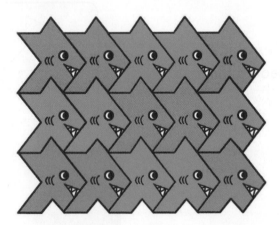

My tessellation is made up of sharks!

Cassie and Ben both designed shapes from a square. The square tessellates, so the new shapes also tessellate.

 **Hands-On Activity**

Material:
• dot paper

Design a shape that tessellates
and make your own tessellation.
Start with a figure that tessellates,
such as one of the shapes below.

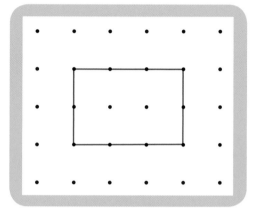 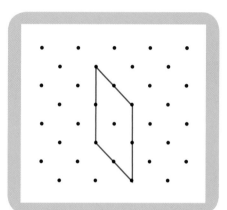

## Guided Learning

**Modify each shape to make a new shape.**
**Then make a tessellation for each new shape.**

**2**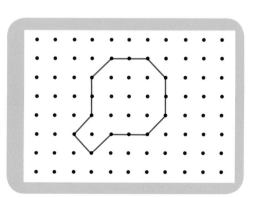

**3**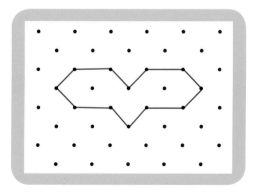

## Let's Practice

**Copy each shape on dot paper.**
**Tessellate each shape in at least two different ways.**

**1**
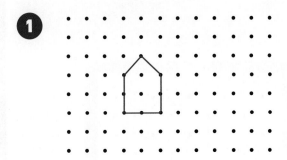

**2**
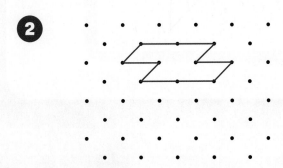

**3**  Start with any shape that tessellates and design a new shape.

**a**  Use the new shape to make a tessellation.
Compare your tessellation with those of your friends.

**b**  Can you use this shape to make another tessellation?

**ON YOUR OWN**

**Go to Workbook B:**
**Practice 2, pages 179–182**

Describe how the second shape is created from the rectangle.
Does it matter how you modify the shape?
Will all modified shapes still tessellate?
Which modifications allow the shape to continue to tessellate
and which do not?

CRITICAL THINKING SKILLS
# Put On Your Thinking Cap!

**PROBLEM SOLVING**

Tech Connection

**WORK IN PAIRS**

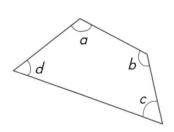

**STEP 1** Use the computer drawing tool to draw any four-sided figure and make twelve copies of it. Your four-sided figure can be different from the one shown.

**STEP 2** Print and cut out the shapes. Then mark the four angles as shown.

**STEP 3** Make a tessellation with the shapes.
Does your figure tessellate?
Why or why not? Explain your answer.

**ON YOUR OWN**

**Go to Workbook B:
Put On Your Thinking Cap!
pages 183–186**

# Chapter Wrap Up

## Study Guide

### You have learned...

## How Tessellations are Formed

A tessellation can be made using a single repeated shape.
This shape covers a surface by extending in all directions with

- no gaps.
- no overlaps.

## Identify Shapes to Make Tessellations

Identify the repeated shape in a tessellation.

Recognize shapes that
- tessellate.
- do not tessellate.

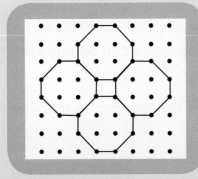

Tessellations can be formed by
- sliding shapes.

- rotating shapes.

- flipping shapes.

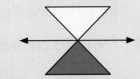

**Tessellations**

### BIG IDEA

▶ A tessellation is made when a shape (or shapes) is repeated, covering a plane (or surface) without gaps or overlaps to form patterns.

## Make Tessellations from Given Shapes

Draw tessellations with a given shape on dot paper.

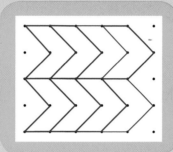

Make different tessellations with a given shape.

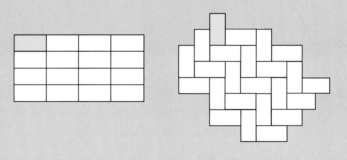

## Modify Shapes to Form New Tessellations

Use a shape that can tessellate to design a new shape that can tessellate.

**Chapter 15**   Tessellations     **285**

# Chapter Review/Test

## Vocabulary

### Choose the correct word.

| tessellation |
| repeated |
| slide |
| rotate |
| flip |
| modify |

**1** When any number of a shape can be fitted together to cover a surface without any gaps or overlaps, a _____ is formed.

**2** A tessellation can be made using a single _____ shape.

**3** To form a tessellation with a given shape, you can _____ or _____ or _____ it.

**4** You can _____ a repeated shape to create a new shape that can tessellate.

## Concepts and Skills

### Identify the repeated shape used to form this tessellation.

**5**

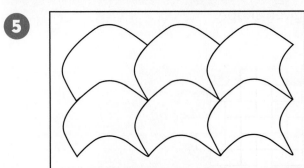

**6** **Copy each shape on dot paper. Identify the shapes that do not tessellate.**

**a**

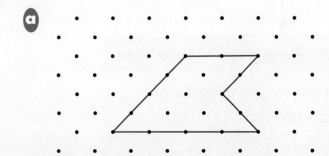

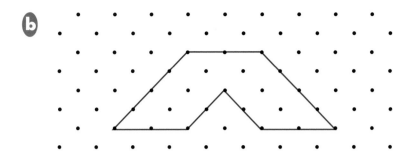

**Copy the shape on dot paper to make two different tessellations.**

**7** Tessellation 1

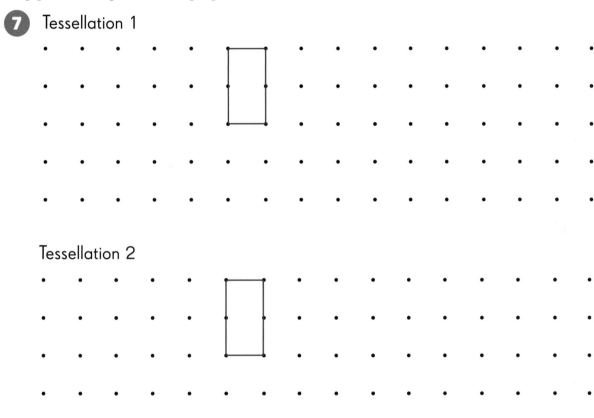

Tessellation 2

**Draw the shape on dot paper. Modify the shape to create a new shape. Then tessellate the new shape.**

**8**

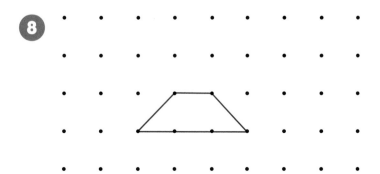

# Glossary

- **acute angle**

  An angle with a measure less than 90°.

  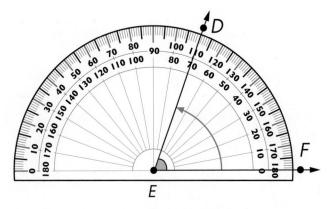

  ∠*DEF* is an acute angle.

- **angle**

  Two rays share the same endpoint form an angle.

  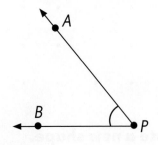

  $\overrightarrow{PA}$ and $\overrightarrow{PB}$ meet to form ∠*APB*.

- **angle measure**

  See *degrees*.

- **area**

   Area is the amount of surface covered by a figure.
   Area can be measured in square units such as
   square centimeter (cm$^2$), square meter (m$^2$), square inch (in.$^2$),
   square foot (ft$^2$), square yard (yd$^2$), and square mile (mi$^2$).

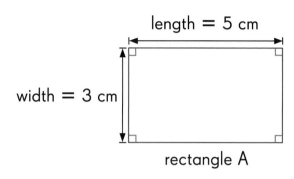

rectangle A

Area of rectangle = length × width
$$= 5 \times 3$$
$$= 15 \text{ cm}^2$$
The area of rectangle A is
15 square centimeters.

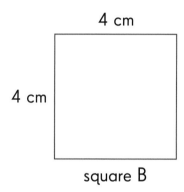

square B

Area of square = length of side ×
length of side
$$= 4 \times 4$$
$$= 16 \text{ cm}^2$$
The area of square B is
16 square centimeters.

B ——————

- **base (of a drawing triangle)**

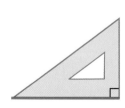

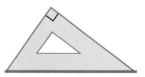

The straightedge is at the base of the drawing triangle.

# C

- **center of rotation**

  See *rotate*.
  centimeter

- **centimeter (cm)**

  A metric unit of distance. $1 \text{ cm} = \frac{1}{100} \text{ m}$

- **clockwise**

  A rotation in the same direction as the hands on a clock.

- **composite figure**

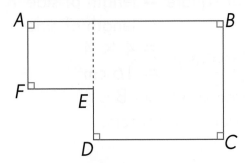

  Figure *ABCDEF* is a composite figure. It can be broken up into a square and a rectangle.

- **congruent**

  Identical parts of figures are congruent. They have the same shape and size.

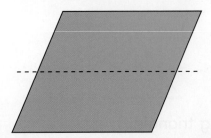

- **counterclockwise**

  A rotation in the opposite direction as the hands on a clock.

- **cup (c)**

  A basic customary unit of capacity.

D

- **decimal**

  A decimal is a way to show amounts that are parts of a whole. A decimal is a number with a decimal point to the right of the ones place, and digits to the right of the decimal point.

  1.52 is a decimal.

- **decimal form**

  1 tenth written in decimal form is 0.1.

- **decimal point**

  A dot or symbol separating the ones and tenths places in a decimal.

  0.1
  ↑
  decimal point

- **degrees (in angles)**

  A unit of angle measure. An angle measure is a fraction of a full turn. The symbol for degrees is °.

  A right angle has a measure of 90 degrees. It can be written as 90°.

- **drawing triangle**

  An instrument used to draw perpendicular and parallel line segments.

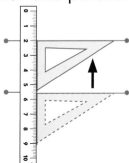

# E ———————

- **endpoint**

  The point at the beginning of a ray or at either end of a line segment.

  ray *AB* or $\overrightarrow{AB}$

  *E* ——————————— *F*

  line segment *EF* or $\overline{EF}$

- **equivalent fraction**

  Equivalent fractions have the same value.

  $\frac{2}{3}$ and $\frac{10}{15}$ are equivalent fractions.

- **expanded form**

  The expanded form of a number shows the number as the sum of the values of its digits.

  $1.46 = 1 + 0.4 + 0.06$

  $1 + 0.4 + 0.06$ is the expanded form of 1.46.

# F ———————

- **flip**

  Turn a shape front to back over a line.

  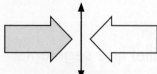

- **fluid ounce (fl oz)**

  A customary unit of capacity. 1 fl oz $= \frac{1}{8}$ cup

- **foot (ft)**

  A basic customary unit of distance.

# G

- **gallon (gal)**

  A customary unit of capacity. 1 gal = 16 cups

- **gram (g)**

  A basic metric unit of mass.

- **greater than (>)**

  Place-value charts can be used to compare decimals.

  | Ones | | Tenths | Hundredths |
  |------|---|--------|------------|
  | 0 | . | 4 | |
  | 0 | . | 3 | 4 |

  0.4 is greater than 0.34.

- **greatest**

  | Ones | | Tenths | Hundredths |
  |------|---|--------|------------|
  | 0 | . | 6 | 2 |
  | 0 | . | 2 | 3 |
  | 0 | . | 6 | 0 |

  The greatest decimal is 0.62.

# H

- **horizontal lines**

   and  are horizontal lines.

  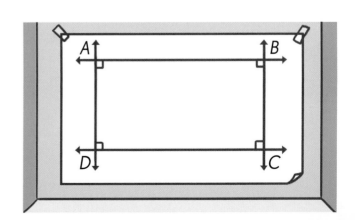

- **hour (h)**

  A unit of time. 1 h = 60 min

- **hundredth**

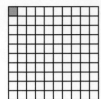

One part out of a hundred is $\frac{1}{100}$ (one hundredth).

# I —————

- **inch (in.)**

  A customary unit of distance. 1 in. $= \frac{1}{12}$ ft

- **inner scale (of a protractor)**

  The inner set of readings on a protractor used for measuring angles.

  Since $\overrightarrow{EF}$ passes through the zero mark of the inner scale, read the measure on the inner scale.

  Measure of $\angle DEF = 70°$

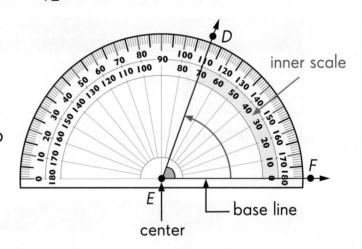

# K —————

- **kilogram (kg)**

  A metric unit of mass. 1 kg $= 1,000$ g

- **kilometer (km)**

  A metric unit of distance. 1 km $= 1,000$ m

# L ——————

- ## least

| Ones | | Tenths | Hundredths |
|:---:|:---:|:---:|:---:|
| 0 | • | 6 | 2 |
| 0 | • | 2 | 3 |
| 0 | • | 6 | 0 |

The least decimal is 0.23.

- ## length

The distance along a line segment or figure from one point to another. It is usually the longer side of a rectangle.

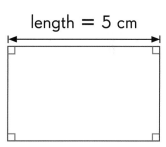

- ## less than (<)

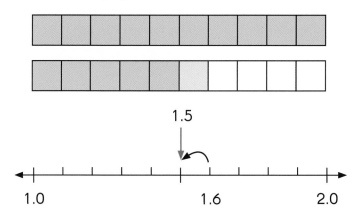

1.5 is 0.1 less than 1.6.

- ## line

A line is a straight path continuing without end in two opposite directions. Write line *CD* or *DC* as $\overleftrightarrow{CD}$ or $\overleftrightarrow{DC}$.

- **line segment**

  A line segment is part of a line with two endpoints.
  Write line segment *EF* or *FE* as $\overline{EF}$ or $\overline{FE}$.

  E •————————————• F

- **line of symmetry**

  A line that divides a figure into
  two congruent parts. The parts match
  exactly when folded along this line.

  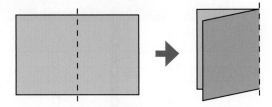

- **line symmetry**

  A figure that can be folded in half so that the halves match exactly
  has line symmetry.

- **liter (L)**

  Liter is a metric unit of volume and capacity. Write L for liter.
  1 L = 1,000 mL

**M**

- **meter (m)**

  A basic unit of distance in the metric system.

- **mile (mi)**

  A customary unit of distance. 1 mi = 5,280 ft

- **milliliter (mL)**

  Milliliter is a metric unit of volume and capacity. Write mL for milliliter.
  1,000 mL = 1 L

- **minute (min)**

  A basic unit of time.

- **modify (a shape)**

  Create a new shape for a tessellation.

  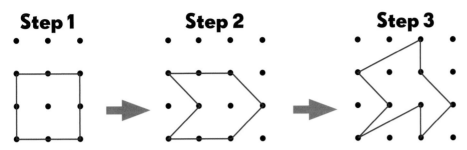

- **more than**

  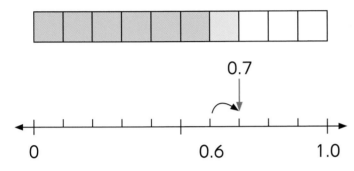

  0.7 is 0.1 more than 0.6.

- **obtuse angle**

  An angle with a measure greater than 90° but less than 180°.

  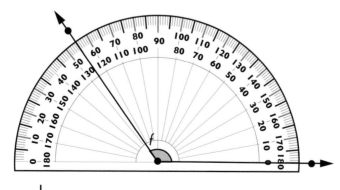

  ∠f is an obtuse angle.

- **order**

  To order a set of numbers is to arrange them in a sequence following a set of rules.

- **ounce (oz)**

  A customary unit of weight. 1 oz $= \frac{1}{16}$ lb

- **outer scale (of a protractor)**

  The outer set of readings on a protractor used for measuring angles.

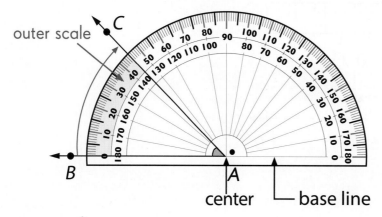

Since $\overrightarrow{AB}$ passes through the zero mark of the outer scale, read the measure on the outer scale.

Measure of $\angle CAB = 45°$

P——————

- **parallel line segments ( ‖ )**

  Parallel line segments are parts of lines that are always the same distance apart.

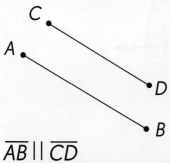

$\overline{AB} \parallel \overline{CD}$

- **perimeter**

  Perimeter is the distance around a figure. Perimeter can be measured in units such as centimeter (cm), meter (m), inch (in.), foot (ft), yard (yd), and mile (mi).

  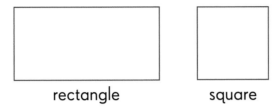

  rectangle          square

  Perimeter of rectangle = length + width + length + width
  Perimeter of square = 4 × length of side

- **perpendicular line segments ( ⊥ )**

  Line segments that meet at right angles.

  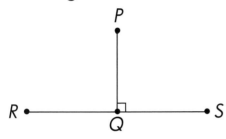

  $\overline{PQ} \perp \overline{RS}$

- **pint (pt)**

  A customary unit of capacity. 1 pt = 2 cups

- **placeholder zero**

  Decimals can have placeholder zeros.
  The digit zero to the right of 9 tenths is a placeholder zero.

  0.9<u>0</u> has the same value as 0.9.
  $$0.9\underline{0} = \frac{90}{100}$$
  $$= \frac{9}{10}$$
  $$= 0.9$$

- **plane**

  A flat surface that extends infinitely in all directions.

- **point**

  An exact location in space represented by a dot.

- **polygon**

  A closed plane figure made by line segments.

- **pound (lb)**

  A basic customary unit of weight.

- **protractor**

  An instrument used to measure and draw angles.

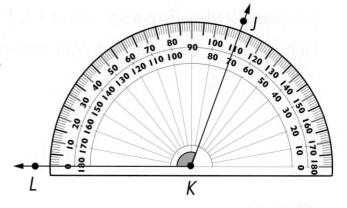

- **quart (qt)**

  A customary unit of capacity. 1 qt = 4 cups

- **ray**

  A ray is part of a line that continues without end in one direction. It has one endpoint.

  Letters can be used to name a ray. The first letter is always the endpoint.

  A ————————→ B          B ————————→ A
  ray *AB*                ray *BA*

  Ray *AB* can also be written as $\overrightarrow{AB}$, and ray *BA* as $\overrightarrow{BA}$.

- **rectangle**

  A rectangle is a four-sided figure with opposite sides parallel, and of equal length.
  It has four right angles.

  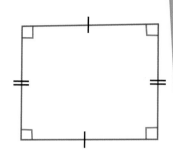

- **repeated shape**

  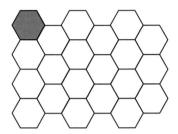

  The repeated shape in this tessellation is .

- **right angle**

  An angle that measures exactly 90°.

- **right triangle**

  A triangle with exactly one right angle.

  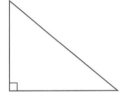

- **rotate**

  The change in position that occurs when a shape is turned about a point. This point is called the *center of rotation*.

  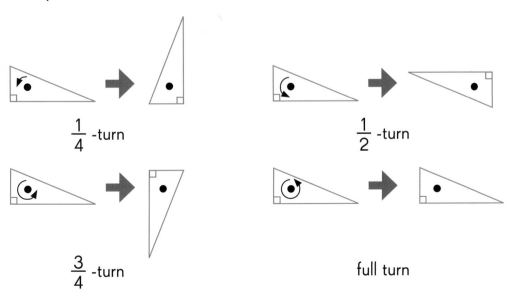

  $\frac{1}{4}$ -turn          $\frac{1}{2}$ -turn

  $\frac{3}{4}$ -turn          full turn

- **rotational symmetry**

  A figure has rotational symmetry if it can be rotated less than a full turn (360°) around a center and look the same as it did before the turn.

  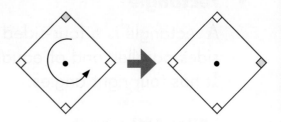

- **round (in decimals)**

  To round a decimal is to express it to the nearest whole number, tenth, and so on.

  5.8 rounded to the nearest whole number is 6.

S ─────────────

- **second (sec)**

  A unit of time. 1 sec = $\frac{1}{60}$ min

- **slide**

  Move a figure in any direction to a new position.

  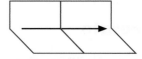

- **square**

  A square is a four-sided figure with four right angles and all sides of equal length. It is a special type of rectangle.

  See *rectangle*.

- **square units**

  Units such as square centimeter (cm²), square meter (m²), square inch (in.²), square foot (ft²), square yard (yd²), and square mile (mi²) are used to measure area.

- **straight angle**

  An angle with a measure of 180°.

   180°

- **symmetric figure (in line symmetry)**

  A figure with two congruent parts that match along the line of symmetry. A figure can have more than one line of symmetry.

- **tenth**

 One part out of ten is $\frac{1}{10}$ (one tenth).

- **tessellation**

  A tessellation can be made using any number of a single repeated shape fitted together to cover a surface without any gap or overlap.

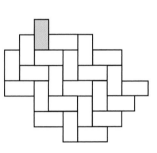

- **turns (and right angles)**

  1 right angle

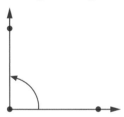

  A $\frac{1}{4}$ -turn is 90°.

  2 right angles

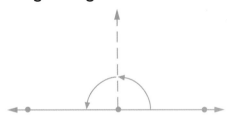

  A $\frac{1}{2}$ -turn is 180°.

  3 right angles

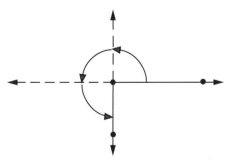

  A $\frac{3}{4}$ -turn is 270°.

  4 right angles

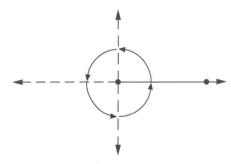

  A full turn is 360°.

- **ton**

  A customary unit of weight. 1 ton = 2,000 lb

- **vertex**

  The point at which two line segments, or rays meet to form an angle.

  Point *P* is called the vertex.

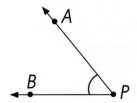

- **vertical lines**

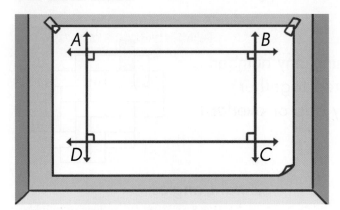

  $\overleftrightarrow{AD}$ and $\overleftrightarrow{BC}$ are vertical lines.

- **width**

  Usually the shorter side of a rectangle.

  See *length*.

  width = 3 cm

- **yard (yd)**

  Yard is a customary unit of length. Write yd for yard. 1 yd = 3 ft

# Index

Pages listed in regular type refer to Student Book A.
Pages in blue type refer to Student Book B.
Pages in *black italic* type refer to Workbook (WB) A pages.
Pages in *blue italic* type refer to Workbook (WB) B pages.
Pages in **boldface** type show where a term is introduced.

rounding, 35–41; *WB 13–16*
subtracting, 65–71, 74–75, 78–79; *WB 27–34*

Decimal form, **4**–79; *WB 1–18*

Decimal point, 4–79; *WB 1–18*

Decompose fractions as a sum in more than one way,
258–263

Degrees
angle measure, 88–109; *WB 48–56*

Denominator of a fraction, **245**

Division
checking, using related multiplication facts, 4–52, 55, 82,
122–125; *WB 21, 37, 63, 65–66*
equation, throughout. *See for example* 116
estimating quotients, *See* Estimation
to find equivalent fractions, 255, 257, 261–263, 266,
269–272, 284; *WB 148, 150, 155, 162, 165–166*
to find a fraction of a number, 276–280, 285–293, 299;
*WB 168–169, 175*
interpreting remainders, 48
inverse operation, 48–51, 55, 65, 67, 122–125, 140;
*WB 21*
modeling
with regrouping, 113–116, 116
one-digit divisors, 113–116, 128–131, 135, 137;
*WB 57–66, 94, 101–102*
quotient, **116**
regrouping in, 113–117, 117–124, 128–131, 135,
136; *WB 57–66, 94*
relationship to multiplication, *See* Relationships
remainder, **116**
to rename improper fractions as mixed numbers, 265–266,
270; *WB 161*
sentence, throughout. *See for example* 49–52, 55, 60,
65, 67, 79, 82, 113–125; *WB 21, 24, 60, 63, 64*
with remainders 117–124; *WB 66, 94*
with regrouping, 111–115
zero in the quotient 118–123; *WB 63–66, 94*

Dollars and cents, 53, 72–75; *WB 14, 25, 33, 34*

Drawing shapes
angles, 86, 93, 109, 145–146, 149, 151, 153;
*WB 51–54*
parallel and perpendicular line segments, 120, 122, 124;
*WB 67–73*

Drawing triangle, 118–122, 127, 130; *WB 69–70, 72–73*

End-of-Year Review, *See* Assessment

Equally likely outcomes, **211**, *See also* Outcomes–likelihood of

Equations (number sentences)
addition/subtraction, *See* Addition *and* Subtraction
bar models and, *See* Bar models
multiplication/division, *See* Multiplication *and* Division
for real-world problems, *See* Algebraic thinking

Equations, unknown angle measure, 98–105

Equivalent fractions
and decimals, 2–3, 42–43, 46–47, 51–52; *WB 2–3,
6, 17–18*
to add and subtract unlike fractions, *See* Fractions

Estimate, *See also* Estimation
versus an exact answer, 67–68, 97; *WB 22*

Estimation
angle measures, 82–84, 91; *WB 49*
and area, 210, 232, 234, 241; *WB 137*
decimals, 35–41; *WB 13–16*
front-end
to estimate differences, **62**, 63, 69, 95–96;
*WB 18–19, 43*
to estimate products, **64**, 65, 96; *WB 20, 43*
to estimate sums, 62, 63, 69, 95–96; *WB 18–19, 43*
to estimate area of a figure, 206–210, 225–226,
232, 234, 241; *WB 137*
using related multiplication facts
to estimate quotients, **65**, 65–67, 69, 96, 134–137,
140; *WB 21, 37, 44, 63, 65–66*
using rounding
to estimate differences, **61**, 63, 69, 95–96;
*WB 17–18, 37, 42*
to estimate products, **63**, 64, 69, 97, 121–124, 138,
149, 140; *WB 19, 43, 55–56*
to estimate sums **60**, 61, 63, 92, 95–96;
*WB 17–18, 42, 48*

Events, *See* Probability

Expanded form, **11**, 12–13, 52–53; 9, 12, 19, 23 *WB 5, 35,*

Pages listed in regular type refer to Student Book A.
Pages in blue type refer to Student Book B.
Pages in *black italic* type refer to Workbook (WB) A pages.
Pages in *blue italic* type refer to Workbook (WB) B pages.
Pages in **boldface** type show where a term is introduced.

Experiment, probability, 214, 218, 220

Exploration
  Let's Explore! 17, 68, 109, 113, 122, 136, 146, 190, 196, 199, 213, 218, 32, 40, 216, 233, 274

Factors, **70**, 71–81, 91, 96–97
  on a multiplication table, 71–76, 83; *WB 23*
  common, 72–75, 79–81, 96; *WB 24, 44*
  greatest common factor, 74–75, 79–80, 96; *WB 25, 44*
Favorable outcome, **216**, *See also* Outcomes and Probability

Find a pattern, 6, 8, 16, 19; *WB 2, 9, 10, 13, 38, 42*

Flip, **271**, 274, 276–277, 284, 286; *WB 185–188, 194*

Formula
  area of a rectangle, 200–201, 205, 224, 226–227, 235, 238; *WB 134–137, 143–146*
  area of a square, 202–203, 205; *WB 134–136, 143–146*

Fractions
  addition with,
      modeling, 245–247, 251, 253, 258, 264–265, 271–273, 280; *WB 147*
  benchmarks, 240–244, 303
  decompose as a sum,
  unlike denominators, 245–247, 280–283, 294, 299; *WB 147–148, 165, 171, 173, 190, 194*
  sums greater than 1, 271–272, 275, 280–281, 292, 259; *WB 165, 173, 195*
  and decimals, 2–3, 42–43, 46–47, 51–52, 44–45, 47, 52; *WB 2–3, 6, 17–18*
  equivalent, 245–250, 271–275, 280–284, 293–295, 299; *WB 147–151*
  to express probability, *See* Probability
  improper, 258–275, 280–283, 286, 293, 298–299; *WB 157–166*
  mixed numbers and, 251–260, 264–275, 280–283, 286, 293, 298–299; *WB 151–156*
  models, *See* Models
  on a number line, 219, 221, 228–229, 254–258, 262–263, 266–268; *WB 154–156*
  numerator and denominator, **245**
  part of a set, *WB 167–170, 178–181, 191*
      modeling, 276–279, 284–293; *WB 167–169, 195, 191*
      representing, 245–250, 261–265, 267–269, 271–293, 276–282, 284–292
  simplest form, 216, **255**, 259, 261–263, 266, 269–272, 284; *WB 155–156, 160, 165–167*
  subtraction with

modeling, 248–250, 273, 282–283, 295; *WB 149*
unlike denominators, 248–250, 269–275, 282–284, 295; *WB 499–150, 166, 176–177, 190, 194*
whole numbers, 273–275, 282–284, 295; *WB 162, 176–173, 195*

Frequency table, *See* Tally chart

Frequency tallies, 140–144

Front-end estimation, 62–65, 69; *WB 18–20, 43*

Full turn, **87**, 98–105, 107, 109; *WB 55–56*

Games, 12, 111, 120, 289, 30, 46, 58, 68

Geometric measurement, *See* Angle measurement, Area, Perimeter

Geometry, *See also* Classifying and Representing
  angles, 80–109; *WB 45–56*
  center, 251–261, 263–265, 270–271, 276, 284; *WB 165–166*
  line, 81, 94–95, 97–98, 107–108, 111–113, 125, 128; *WB 71–74*
  line segment, 81–84, 114–124, 126–130; *WB 67–70*
  ray, 85–86, 88–97, 99, 107–109; *WB 45–50*
  parallel lines, 110–115, 121–124, 99–130
  perpendicular lines, 110–120, 99–130
  shape patterns, 267, 269–275
  symmetry, 242–265; *WB 163–169*
  tessellations, 243–287; *WB 173–194*
  rotations, 251–261, 263–265, 270–271, 276, 284; *WB 165–166, 169, 185–186*
  turns, 87, 98–107, 109; *WB 55–56*

Glossary, 303–321, 288–304

Graphs
  bar, using, 149–152, 165, 167–169, 175; *WB 80, 95*
  line, 159–164, 167–169, 177; *WB 85–87, 89–90, 99–100*
  pictographs, 166–169; *WB 88*
  selecting appropriate, 165–149; *WB 88*

Gram, 166–178

Grid paper
  drawing symmetric shapes, 145, 148; *WB 167–169*
  estimating area, 206–210, 225–226, 232, 234, 241; *WB 137*

Guided Practice, *See* Practice

Pages listed in regular type refer to Student Book A.
Pages in blue type refer to Student Book B.
Pages in *black italic* type refer to Workbook (WB) A pages.
Pages in *blue italic* type refer to Workbook (WB) B pages.
Pages in **boldface** type show where a term is introduced.

subtraction

  with fractions, 248–250, 273, 282–283, 295;
    *WB 187*
  with decimals, 65–66, 69, 73–75, 79
  tenths and hundredths, 2–7, 11, 13–14, 16, 18, 21,
    24–25, 42–45, 47; *WB 1, 3, 5*

Modify

  in tessellation, **278**–283, 285, 287; *WB 190*

Money

  decimal form, 53, 72–75; *WB 14, 25, 33, 34*

More likely outcome, 210, *See also* Outcomes–likelihood of

Multiples, **68**, 89–91, 96

  common, **70**, 71, 89, 75; *WB 31, 39, 45*
  least common, **70**, 71–89, 83; *WB 36, 45*
  on a multiplication table, 73–77, 67–70; *WB 29–31, 45*

Multiplication

  area models, 74–76
  array, 74–76, 92–100
  as a comparison, 68–73
  commutative property, 73
  equations, throughout. *See for example* 92–100, 101–110
  estimating products, 63–65, 69, 96, 107–98, 124, 135,
    140; *WB 19, 20, 43, 55–56*
  to find equivalent fractions, 245–250, 267–269,
    271–275; *WB 147–150, 161–166*
  to find a fractional part of a number, 278–279; *WB 170,
    180, 181*
  to find a fraction of a set, 278–279, 285–293, 299;
    *WB 174, 180–181*
  inverse operations, 49–52, 55, 65, 67, 120–123, 140;
    *WB 21*
  modeling, 57, 94–95, 101
  by multiples of 10 and 100, 101–103, 109; *WB 55–56*
  by one-digit numbers, 94–100, 124, 137; *WB 51–54, 93*
  product, 94–110, 124–124, 132, 135–136, 137
  regrouping in, 94–99, 124–132, 132, 135–136, 137;
    *WB 51–58, 93*
  relationship to division, 49–52, 55
  by two-digit numbers, 103–113, 109, 132, 135–136,
    137; *WB 55–58, 93*
  sentence, throughout. *See for example* 47–52, 69,
    70–75, 65, 65–68, 88, 92, 94, 94, 95–96, 98,
    103; *WB 20, 22, 51–58, 93*

Multiplicative comparison, 68–73

Multi-step problems

  solving, 126–135, 140; *WB 67–69*
  modeling, 126–135, 140; *WB 69, 73*

Naming geometric shapes, 132–136

Number cubes, 97, 267

Number line

  to compare, 33; *WB 9*
  to estimate, 107–110
  to model equivalent fractions, 255, 258, 262–263, 298
  to show probability, **219**, 221, 228–229; *WB 128,
    139–140*
  to model decimals, 3–8, 11, 13–14, 16, 18, 21–22,
    24–27, 35–43, 47; *WB 2, 6, 9, 10, 13, 15*

Numbers to 100,000

  comparing, 14–20, 33, 54–69, 90; *WB 7–13, 14,
    41–42*
  expanded form, **11**, 12–13, 35–36; *WB 5, 41*
  ordering, **15**, 18; *WB 7–8, 42*
  patterns, **6**, 8, 16, 19; *WB 2, 9, 10, 13, 38, 42*
  standard form, **6**, 7–9, 35–36; *WB 1, 41*
  word form, **6**, 7–9, 35–36; *WB 1, 41*

Number patterns, 6, 8, 16, 19; *WB 2, 9, 10, 13, 38, 42*
  decimals, 26–30, 34, 52; *WB 10, 12*

Number sense

  common multiples, **70**, 71, 73, 99; *WB 31, 39, 45*
  comparing whole numbers, 14–20, 33, 60–62, 90;
    *WB 7–13, 16, 41–42*
  front-end estimation, *See* Estimation
  interpreting remainders, 49
  multiplication and division, *See* Multiplication *and* Division

Number sentences

  addition/subtraction, *See* Addition *and* Subtraction
  bar models and, *See* Bar models
  multiplication/division, *See* Multiplication *and* Division
  for real-world problems, *See* Algebraic thinking

Number theory

  factors, *See* Factors
  multiples, *See* Multiples
  prime and composite numbers, 62, 63, 66, 99;
    *WB 26–28, 45*

Numerator of a fraction, **245**

Pages listed in regular type refer to Student Book A.
Pages in blue type refer to Student Book B.
Pages in *black italic* type refer to Workbook (WB) A pages.
Pages in *blue italic* type refer to Workbook (WB) B pages.
Pages in **boldface** type show where a term is introduced.

Obtuse angle, **90**–93, 97, 108–109; *WB 48, 53*

Operations, *See* Addition, Division, Multiplication, *and* Subtraction

Opposite sides (of a rectangle), 132, 134, 136–138, 143, 146–147, 151–152; *WB 79–87*

Ordering
    data, 193–194, 196, 202, 205; *WB 111–112,*
        *See also* Line plot and Stem-and-leaf plot
    whole numbers, **15**, 18; *WB 7–8, 42*
    decimals, 29–30, 52; *WB 12*

Organizing data
    line plot, *See* Line plot
    stem-and-leaf plot, *See* Stem-and-leaf plot
    table, 145–158, 164, 173–176; *WB 77–83, 95–98*
    tally chart, 147–148, 150, 174; *WB 77, 73*

Ounce, 166–178

Outcomes
    likelihood of, 210–213, 215, 219–221, 227–228;
        *WB 123–124, 139–140, 192, 197*
    meaning of, **210**
    probability of, 216–221, 228–229, 232–233, 238;
        *WB 125–128, 139–141, 146, 193, 199*

Outer scale (on a protractor), 88, 90–93, 107–109; *WB 47*

Outlier, **207**, 226–227; *WB 119, 122, 136, 192, 198*

Parallel lines, 111–113, 125, 128

Parallel line segments, 110, 116, 121–124, 126–130;
    *WB 69–72, 71–73*

Patterns
    completing, 6, 8, 16, 19; *WB 2, 9, 10, 13, 38, 42*
    creating, 16; *WB 9*
    decimals, 26–30, , 52; *WB 10, 12*
    extending, 6, 8, 16, 19; *WB 2, 9, 10, 13, 38, 42*
    numerical, 6, 8, 16, 19; *WB 2, 9, 10, 13, 38, 42*
    rules, 2–4, 14–19
    shape, 267–268, 269–275, 276–282
    symmetric, 256, 258–263, 265; *WB 168–169*
    wallpaper, 154

Perimeter
    of a square, 212–213, 215, 217, 238, 240; *WB 135,*
        *139–141, 145*
    of a rectangle, 211–215, 217, 238, 240; *WB 135, 139,*
        *141–142, 145*
    of a composite figure, 218–219, 222, 223, 230–231,
        234–236, 239, 241; *WB 147–149, 155*

Perpendicular lines, 107–113, 125, 128

Perpendicular line segments, 110, 116–120, 126–132;
    *WB 67–68, 71–73*

Pictographs, 166–169; *WB 88*

Placeholder zero, **17**–18, *WB 8, 10, 12, 15–16*

Place value to 100,000, **10**
    comparing numbers, 14–20, 33, 60–62, 90; *WB 7–13,*
        *16, 41–42*
    hundred thousand, **8**
    ten thousand, **5**, 6–37; *WB 2–5, 15–16, 41–42, 48*
    ordering numbers, 15, 18; *WB 7–8, 42*

Place-value chart, **5**, 6–7, 9–10, 12, 14–16, 18, 93–95,
    97–98, 101, 113–116, 6–9, 11–12, 14–19, 22–23,
    28–29, 32, 34, 54–57, 59, 61–62, 65–66, 69; *WB 1,*
    *4–5, 11*

Place-value blocks, 86–91, 93

Plots
    line plot, *See* Line plot
    stem-and-leaf plot, *See* Stem-and-leaf plot

Point, 4–12, 159–169

Polygons, 243–265, *WB 163–165, 167–168, 170*

Pound, 166–178

Practice
    Guided Practice, throughout. *See for example* 7–8,
        10–11, 15–16, 45–51, 54, 57–59, 5–6, 7–10,
        14, 16–21, 25–26, 29, 37, 39, 43–46
    Let's Practice, throughout. *See for example* 9, 13, 18–19,
        69, 65–66, 89, 99–100, 109–110, 11–12, 27–28,
        34, 41, 47, 64, 71, 75, 93, 97, 105

Predict
    likelihood of an outcome, 210–212, 215, 219–221,
        227–228; *WB 123–124, 139–140, 192, 197*

Prerequisite skills
    Recall Prior Knowledge 2–3, 40–42, 85–90, 140–142,

Pages listed in regular type refer to Student Book A.
Pages in blue type refer to Student Book B.
Pages in *black italic* type refer to Workbook (WB) A pages.
Pages in *blue italic* type refer to Workbook (WB) B pages.
Pages in **boldface** type show where a term is introduced.

# Photo Credits

cover: ©Krys Bailey/Alamy, cover: ©Tom Uhlman/ Alamy. Image provided by Houghton Mifflin Harcourt, 2: ©Jani Bryson/iStock, 3t: ©Jani Bryson/iStock, 3b: ©Stockbyte Photo CD, 4: ©Stockbyte Photo CD, 5: ©Stockbyte Photo CD, 6: ©Stockbyte/Getty Images, 7: ©aabejon/iStock, 9: ©Aldo Murillo/iStock, 13: ©Jani Bryson/iStock, 16: ©Quavondo/iStock, 21: ©Maica/ iStock, 26t: ©Mamahoohooba/Dreamstime.com, 26b: ©Image Source Limited, 28: ©Thomas Perkins/ iStock, 29t: ©Stockbyte Photo CD, 29b: ©Image Source Limited, 32: ©parfyonov/iStock, 33t: ©Aldo Murillo/iStock, 33b: ©Sean Locke/iStock, 35t: ©Joeb/ morgueFile.com, 35b: ©aabejon/iStock, 36: ©aabejon/ iStock, 42: ©Image Source Limited, 43t: ©Image Source Limited, 43b: ©Stockbyte Photo CD, 44t: ©Vikram Raghuvanshi/iStock, 44b: © Image Source Limited, 45t: ©aabejon/iStock, 45m: ©aabejon/iStock, 45b: ©Aldo Murillo/iStock, 49: ©Thomas Perkins/ iStock, 56: ©aabejon/iStock, 61: ©Sean Locke/iStock, 63: ©Stockbyte/Getty Images, 65: ©Quavondo/ iStock, 66: ©Jani Bryson/iStock, 73: ©Image Source Limited, 80: ©Rui G. Santos/Dreamstime.com, 82: ©aabejon/iStock, 85: ©Stockbyte Photo CD, 86: ©Gisele/iStock, 88t: ©Aldo Murillo/iStock, 88b: ©aabejon/iStock, 90: ©Image Source Limited, 94: ©aabejon/iStock, 95: ©Image Source Limited, 99: ©Image Source Limited, 102: ©Mamahoohooba/ Dreamstime.com, 105t: ©MCE, 105b: ©MCE, 112: ©MCE, 113l: ©Simfo/iStock, 113m: ©Jamalludin Bin Abu Seman Din/Dreamstime.com, 113r: ©Diane Diederich/iStock, 116: ©dorne/morgueFile.com, 118: ©aabejon/iStock, 122: © aabejon/iStock, 125: ©Image Source Limited, 126: ©MCE, 127: ©Aldo Murillo/ iStock, 135: © Image Source Limited, 136: ©Image Source Limited, 140: ©Image Source Limited, 145: ©parfyonov/iStock, 148: ©Image Source Limited, 161: ©aabejon/iStock, 162t: ©Mamahoohooba/ Dreamstime.com, 162b: ©Aldo Murillo/iStock, 163t: ©Image Source Limited, 163b: ©Sean Locke/iStock, 168t: ©Mamahoohooba/Dreamstime.com, 168b: ©Stockbyte/Getty Images, 172: ©aabejon/iStock, 200t: ©Gisele/iStock, 200b: ©Stockbyte Photo CD, 201t: ©Image Source Limited, 201b: ©Maica/iStock, 202: ©parfyonov/iStock, 211: ©Aldo Murillo/iStock, 212: ©Stockbyte Photo CD, 215: ©Image Source Limited, 220: ©Mamahoohooba/Dreamstime.com, 226l: ©dorne/morgueFile.com  226r: ©MCE, 227: ©Image Source Limited, 236: ©aabejon/iStock, 242tl: ©Schick / morgueFile.com, 242tr: ©More Pixels/ iStock, 242bl: ©MCE, 242br: ©Feng Yu/Dreamstime. com, 243l: ©Digital Stock, 243r: ©John Clines/iStock, 245: ©aabejon/iStock, 246: ©Thomas Perkins/iStock, 247: © Aldo Murillo/iStock, 248: ©Thomas Perkins/ iStock, 251: ©Image Source Limited, 252: ©Image Source Limited, 253: ©Quavondo/iStock, 269: ©MCE, 270: ©Sean Locke/iStock, 271: ©Stockbyte Photo CD, 274: ©Stockbyte Photo CD, 276: ©Aldo Murillo/ iStock, 278: ©Mamahoohooba/Dreamstime.com, 279: ©Mamahoohooba/Dreamstime.com, 280: ©Gisele/ iStock

# Acknowledgements

The publisher wishes to thank the following organizations for sponsoring the various objects used in this book:

**Growing Fun Pte Ltd**
Base-ten cubes and blocks – appear throughout the book

**Noble International Pte Ltd**
Unit cubes p. 185

The publisher also wishes to thank the individuals who have contributed in one way or another and all those who have kindly loaned the publisher items for the photographs featured.